TECI TAILGATES

GOOD FOOD TO GOBBLE UP ON GAME DAY

KIRSTEN TITLAND
MELISSA MONCRIEF COBBLER

©2004 AUDREY LYNN PUBLISHING, LLC

Published By:
Audrey Lynn Publishing, LLC
P.O. Box 10041
Blacksburg, VA 24062

ISBN No. 0-9759341-0-4

Proudly printed in the United States of America by:
Jamont Communications
Leaders in Electronic &
Traditional Print Technology
Boyd Johnson, President
339 W. Luck Avenue
Roanoke, VA 24016
P.O. Box 331, Roanoke, VA 24003-0331
Telephone (540) 345-9867
Fax (540) 345-1689
(800) 722-0786

TABLE OF CONTENTS

INTRODUCTION

As Virginia Tech alumni and avid Hokie football fans, we look forward to the fall when we gather with family and friends, put on the Orange and Maroon, and cheer the Hokies to victory. It is a tradition that brings us together to renew friendships, relive old times and make new memories, all while enjoying good food.

Longtime friends and college roommates, we often shared tailgating recipes and entertaining ideas. After the 2003 football season, we decided to bring together our experiences and ideas to write a cookbook for Virginia Tech tailgaters.

With the help of friends and family, we put together this book of tips, menus, and easy recipes to enrich the tailgating experience of Hokie fans everywhere. Whether you're a seasoned tailgater or new to the game, Tech Tailgates covers the field with a variety of delicious, crowd-pleasing recipes. Included are traditional tailgating recipes as well as some ideas that may start new traditions at your football party. The Game Plan section will walk you through the steps of organizing a party from kickoff to the 4th quarter.

We hope this book will help you entertain Tech fans in true Hokie style. Our friend Ginger Edwards, class of '86 said it best, *"It's really more about getting together with friends and fellow Hokies than it is the food. Don't get me wrong, the food is DELICIOUS but the friendships are even better."*

GO HOKIES!

Melissa Moncrief Cobbler is a 1992 graduate of Virginia Tech with a B.A. in Urban Affairs and a Masters in Healthcare Administration from the University of South Carolina. Melissa and her husband, Ken (also a '92 Tech graduate) recently returned to Roanoke after being away for several years. They are passing down their love for the Hokies and tailgating to their children, Madeline and Mason, and never miss a home game.

Kirsten Titland is a 1993 graduate of Virginia Tech with a B.S. in Dietetics and a second B.S. in Nutrition. Kirsten lives, works, and plays in the Blacksburg area. She has spent much of the last ten years creating culinary extravaganzas for friends and family, using quality and love as her main ingredients.

ACKNOWLEDGEMENTS

We wish to thank our friends and family for their contributions and support in the making of this book. We especially would like to thank:

Ken Cobbler
Wayne and Linda Cobbler
Minta Getzen
Boyd Johnson
Kathy Johnston
Horace and Vicki Moncrief
Robin Nalepa
Barbara Titland

This book is dedicated to
Hokie Fans
everywhere!

GAME PLAN

THE GAME PLAN

Planning a tailgate party, or having some Hokies over to watch the game? A good football coach will tell you, it is always best to have a game plan. Here are some helpful tips to make your tailgate effortless, and keep you out of the kitchen on game day.

First, make a list of who you are expecting to join your game day feast and add a few more. You never know who might stop by.

Once you know how many hungry fans to feed, decide on a theme and menu. Some tailgaters try to stay ahead of the game and plan each tailgate party well before the season opener, others decide from week to week. Whichever is your game plan, a theme allows you and your tailgating crew to create a fun, tasty menu. Many of our recipes celebrate our Gobbler traditions, such as grilled turkey legs and can be included in a Hokie themed menu. Or on the contrary, choose a menu that is characteristic of Tech opponents.

We had a huge spread for the LSU game in true New Orleans fashion with jambalaya, Cajun shrimp, and beignets. It was a great opportunity to serve something we wouldn't ordinarily have.

You can also pick a theme based on the time of day or the time of year. Why not go for a brunch tailgate, a traditional barbeque, or, perhaps a mini-Oktoberfest? The possibilities are endless and anything goes.

There is only one rule when it comes to tailgating good food and lots of it!

A week before, plan your grocery list. Read each recipe so you can create a preparation timeline. For example, some recipes freeze well and can be made up to a week in advance. Others may need to marinate for at least 24 hours, or just taste better the next day. Remember that tailgating is a group effort and a season-long potluck. Coordinate with your friends. There is no need for one person to prepare everything.

Make a run to the grocery store several days before game day. Have you ever tried to make a quick run to the Blacksburg Kroger on game day? It is best to stock up in advance.

Once you have your ingredients, start cooking! Prepare as many foods in advance as you can. So when you wake up, you can cook or reheat while you get ready.

The day of the big game is also a day for last minute details. When entertaining at home, finish any food preparation, and set the table *buffet style*. Make sure you have your serving dishes out and any hot plates you may need. Get the T.V. room ready for your company and put on the Orange and Maroon. If you are headed to Lane Stadium, our tailgating tips will steer you in the right direction.

TAILGATING TIPS

Once you have planned your menu, make a list of any special utensils, storage containers, and cooking equipment you will need. A well thought out checklist will make for an effortless tailgate. We have taken some of the guesswork out of it and created two for you on pages 13 and 14. The first list is for items to pack the night before and the second list is for items to pack on game day. Pack your vehicle with items in reverse order of how you will use them. The first thing you need at the tailgate should be the last thing you pack in the car.

We tailgate with the same group of friends every week. Before the season opener, we assign items for everyone to bring. Disposable plates, cups, napkins, and other necessities are then placed in our "tailgate box" which one couple brings to every game after that. We may have to add some special items week to week depending on what we are serving, but it saves time and usually lasts all season.

Store prepared foods in convenient containers when tailgating. For example, cut fresh vegetables the night before and put in plastic bags so that all you have to do when you get to the game is dump them in a serving bowl. Place secure lids on dips, sauces and any spill-prone items.

Now that you have your supplies, the most important thing is keeping cold foods cold and hot foods hot.

Keeping it Cold
Pack a cooler just for beverages. Drinks made in large batches can be served from beverage coolers. It is a fun and convenient way to keep your tailgaters happy. Be sure to pack extra ice to keep drinks cold.

Pack a separate cooler for food items that need to be kept cold. Keep in mind that **raw meats need to be kept at 40° or less**. In addition, keep meats sealed in plastic bags to prevent leakage to other items.

We suggest, when possible, splitting a perishable item, such as potato salad, into 2 containers. Store one in the cooler and serve the other. After 2 hours, rotate the containers throwing the used one away.

Keeping it Hot
Yes, you can have hot food at a tailgate without a grill! And here's how:

Heat the food or drink at home to a very hot temperature before you leave.

If you have a hard plastic cooler or thermos, fill it with boiling water, let stand for a few minutes, empty, then, add your food or drink. Keep the container closed until time to serve. Soup or chili can be served directly from a clean cooler. Just be sure that you don't fill it too closely to the top.

Foil lined insulated coolers work very well for warm sandwiches, casseroles, and other foods. Take items directly from the oven or stove, carefully wrap in a kitchen towel, if necessary, (to avoid melting any soft plastic) and place inside. Zip up the cooler and open only when time to serve.

We had a package of Touchdown Rolls (pg.82) that were still warm after the game when stored in this way.

Chafing dishes are a great tailgating accessory to keep food warm during the festivities. The gel formula cooking fuel is more practical to travel with and will keep your food at 140°. Be sure to bring water for your chafing dish.

Timing is Everything

When planning your tailgate, remember to allow time to set up, clean up, and walk to the stadium. (It is quite a hike from the Duck Pond.) That way you can enjoy all the fun in between and be in your seat and ready for kickoff. Plenty of trash bags and antibacterial wipes will help you clean up your party quickly. Help keep Tech's campus looking great!

GRILLING GUIDELINES

Grilling at the game has never been easier with the portable gas grills now on the market. Available at home improvement stores, they are relatively lightweight and can cook a large amount of food. We have tested the Weber and have been pleased with its performance. Make sure you have the right connectors for your gas tank and read the instructions *before* game day.

A few grilling rules for the guys:
Grill with the lid down. It allows the grill to cook your food more evenly.

Take your aggression out on the field, not on your food! Unless the recipe calls for it, flip your food only once and don't poke it or smash it with a spatula. You only lose flavor.

Make sure you turn your grill off before going into the game and allow sufficient time to cool before reloading it into your vehicle.

Whether you are roasting in the oven or cooking over hot coals, every meat should be cooked to a certain temperature for safety. Make sure you have a meat thermometer, and check the temperature in the thickest part of the meat, careful not to poke all the way through.

Approximate grill times:

Chicken Breast	8-12 min	Medium Heat
Beef Burgers	8-10 min	Medium Heat
Turkey Drumstick	3/4-11/4 hr	Low Heat
Pork Tenderloin	25-30 min	Medium Heat
Bratwurst	25-30 min	Low Heat
Shrimp	2-5 min	High Heat

Internal cooking temperatures:

Meat	Internal cooking temperature
Chicken	160-170°
Turkey	170-180°
Pork	160°
Beef	
Rare	125°
Med-Rare	145°
Medium	160°
Well	170°
Hamburger	160°
Turkeyburger	165°

SAFETY

Keep raw meats at 40° or cooler. Seal them in plastic bags to prevent leakage to other items in the cooler.

Use a meat thermometer and cook meat to the proper internal temperature!

Once perishable food has been sitting out for more than 2 hours, toss it (1 hour for those rare 90° days in Blacksburg).

Raw meat requires its own cutting board. We recommend bringing disposable cutting boards which are now available at your local grocery store.

Be sure to turn off your grill and extinguish any sternos before heading into the game.

Be a responsible tailgater and assign a designated driver when necessary.

Do not, under any circumstances, park beside Lee Corso. Lightning has been known to strike the same place twice!

TAILGATING CHECKLIST

Pack your car the night before with these essential items in *reverse* order of how you will use them.

- ❏ **Jumper cables** – *it happens to the best of us!*
- ❏ **First Aid Kit**
- ❏ **Extra layers of clothing, hats, gloves**
- ❏ **Rain gear** – *remember Hurricane Isabel?!*
- ❏ **Sunglasses**
- ❏ **Sunscreen** – *be sure to apply extra sunscreen to the one side of your face that always seems to burn!*
- ❏ **Resealable bags**
- ❏ **Trash bags**
- ❏ **Wet wipes**
- ❏ **Paper towels**
- ❏ **Napkins**
- ❏ **Lighter/matches**
- ❏ **Spatula or tongs**
- ❏ **Meat thermometer**
- ❏ **Disposable cutting board(s)**
- ❏ **Chafing dish or other cooking equipment**
- ❏ **Sharp kitchen knife**
- ❏ **Serving pieces e.g. ladle**
- ❏ **Disposable forks, knives, spoons**
- ❏ **Disposable cups, plates, and bowls**
- ❏ **Folding chairs**
- ❏ **Tablecloth** – *maroon and orange, of course!*
- ❏ **Folding table(s)**
- ❏ **Bottle opener/corkscrew**
- ❏ **Grill w/ full tank of gas and connectors**
- ❏ **Hokie tailgating tent**

GAME DAY CHECKLIST

- ❑ **Football tickets and parking pass**
- ❑ **Drinks cooler with extra ice**
- ❑ **Water** – for drinking, washing, putting out fires
- ❑ **Cold food cooler**
- ❑ **Warm food cooler**
- ❑ **Car magnets and flags**
- ❑ **Hokie Fans**

Don't worry if you forget something. Hokie tailgaters are always prepared to help someone in need!

MENU IDEAS

We have put together these menus as a guide to help you plan your football feast. Tailgating should be fun and stress free. You can always order party platters for convenience to add to your homemade creations.

Summertime Tailgate
Deviled Eggs with a Kick
Inn at Riverbend Texas Caviar
Veggies with Ranch Dip
Grilled Herb Chicken
Pepper Steak Slices
Garlic Rosemary Potatoes
Broccoli Salad
Raspberry Almond Bars
Goal Line Brownies
Southgate Sangria

Virginia Tech vs. NC State
Spinach Dip
Running Back Dip
Burruss Hall Beef BBQ
Relish Salad
Traditional Potato Salad
Irene's Beans
Grilled Fruit Skewers
Brown Sugar Poundcake
Fruited Tea

Autumn Breakfast Buffet Tailgate
Cinnamon Stewed Apples
Mini Cinnamon Rolls
Touchdown Rolls
Sausage, Egg, and Cheese Tarts
Orange and Maroon Loaf
Fresh Fruit Salad with Poppy Seed Dressing*
Highty Tighty Hot Chocolate
Mimosas

Poppy Seed Dressing: 1cup vanilla yogurt, 3 tbsp. honey, 1 tbsp. poppy seeds

Virginia Tech vs. Maryland
Seasoned Oyster Crackers
Game Winning Cheese Dip
Cream Cheese Crab Spread
Traditional Coleslaw
Old Bay Fries
Mini Maryland Crabcakes
Extra Point Chicken
Turtle Brownies*
Sea Breeze Punch

Brownies: Prepare store-bought brownies according to package directions. Serve with caramel sauce, chopped pecans and whipped topping.

Tex Mex
Goal Line Guacamole
Cheesy Salsa Dip
Tortilla Chips
Mexican Rollups
Black Bean Wraps
Chicken Quesadillas
Coconut Cream Cheese Pound Cake
with strawberries
Chocolate Surprise Cookies
Yummy Margaritas

Virginia Tech vs. Georgia Tech
Pecan Spread
Hot Ham-n-Cheese Rolls
Stuff the Quarterback Mushrooms
Brunswick Stew for a Crowd
Blue Cheese Bites
Peach Bowl Crisp
Pecan Pie Bars
Fuzzy Blue Gobblers

Virginia Tech vs. Miami
Green Chile-Cheese Dip
Enchilada Stacks
Cuban Black Bean Soup
Pimento Cheese Sandwiches
Key Lime Squares
Crescent School Cookies
Beat the Hurricanes Punch

Oktoberfest
Seasoned Pretzels
Hokie Sandwich Bites
Grilled Beer Bratwurst
with green peppers, onions, and sauerkraut
Twice Baked Potatoes
Pumpkin Pie Dip
with apple slices and gingersnaps
Goal Line Brownies
German Beer
Warm n' Cozy Gobblers

Virginia Tech vs. UVA
Apricot Brie
Onion Soufflé
Hot Spinach-Artichoke Dip
Baked Potato Soup
Turkey Cranberry Croissants
Orange and Maroon Salad
Tech Toffee Bites
Pumpkin Bread
Hot Spiced Cider

KICKOFF

BRUNCH
&
BREAKFAST

There's no better way to kickoff an early game day tailgate than with a crowd pleasing brunch. In this chapter we feature winning casseroles, breads, spreads, and more. Score points with your team when you serve up the Quarterback's Casserole, an All-American family favorite. The Orange and Maroon Loaf adds a splash of Hokie color to any table.

Quarterback's Casserole

Like any good game plan, this dish has to be prepared in advance. It is one of our family favorites!

2 cups frozen hash browns	10 eggs, beaten
1 cup flavored croutons	2 cups half & half
1/4 cup chopped onion	Dash salt
3 cups Cheddar cheese, shredded	1/4 tsp. cayenne
1 lb. sausage, fully cooked and crumbled	1 cup crushed corn flakes

In a 13 x 9 baking dish, layer potatoes, croutons, onions, half the cheese, and sausage; top with remaining cheese and set aside. In a large bowl, blend eggs, milk, and seasonings. Pour over layers. Cover and refrigerate overnight. Remove from refrigerator and let sit 15 minutes before baking. Sprinkle corn flakes over top. Bake in preheated oven at 350° for 45 minutes or until set. Let stand 5 minutes before serving.

Makes 10 to 12 servings

Pre-Game Breakfast Pizza

This pizza can be made the night before and reheated the morning of the game for a quick and hearty breakfast.

1 (8 oz.) can crescent
  roll dough
1 1/2 cup chopped ham
1 cup frozen hash brown
  potatoes, thawed
1 cup shredded Cheddar
  cheese

5 eggs
1/4 cup milk
1/4 tsp. salt
1/8 tsp. pepper

Roll out crescent dough onto a 15 x 10 baking pan. Press all seams together. Sprinkle ham, hash browns and cheese over dough. In a large mixing bowl, whisk together eggs, milk, salt and pepper. Pour egg mixture over ham, hash browns and cheese. Spread evenly and bake at 375° for 30 minutes, or until golden brown and bubbly. Let sit for 10 minutes before serving.

Makes 6 to 8 servings

French Toast Casserole

This is the perfect recipe to use up that 'days old' French bread loaf. The rest of the ingredients are usually on hand. It is best to prepare the night before—just throw in the oven the next morning.

1/2 **cup butter, melted**	**6 eggs**
1 cup firmly packed	**1**1/2 **cup milk**
brown sugar	**2 tsp. vanilla extract**
1 loaf French bread,	1/2 **tsp. cinnamon**
few days old,	**Powdered sugar**
cut into 1" slices	

Mix together butter and brown sugar with an electric mixer. Spread mixture evenly on the bottom of a 13 x 9 baking dish. Place French bread slices on top of butter and sugar mix. Set aside. In a large mixing bowl, whisk together eggs, milk, vanilla and cinnamon. Pour over bread slices and refrigerate 6 hours to overnight. Remove from refrigerator and let sit on countertop for 30 minutes before baking. Preheat oven to 350°. Bake casserole for 45 minutes, or until golden brown. Let sit for 5 minutes. Sprinkle with powdered sugar.

Makes 8 to 10 servings

Sausage, Egg, and Cheese Tarts

An easy finger food for a party at home or on the tailgate buffet.

1/2 **lb. pork sausage,**
   cooked and crumbled
1 1/4 **cups biscuit mix**
1/4 **cup butter or**
   margarine, melted
2 **tbsp. boiling water**

1 **egg, beaten**
1/2 **cup half and half**
2 **tbsp. thinly sliced**
   green onions
1/2 **cup shredded**
   Cheddar cheese

Combine biscuit mix, butter, and boiling water; stir well forming a dough. Press about 1 tablespoon of dough into bottom and up sides of well greased and floured regular sized muffin tin. Spoon sausage evenly into cups. In a small bowl, combine egg, half and half, and green onions; stir well. Spoon about 1 tablespoon of the egg mixture into each cup. Bake at 375° for 20 minutes. Sprinkle cheese over each tart; bake an additional 5 minutes.

Makes 12 tarts

Baked Oatmeal

A heartwarming breakfast dish that is delicious served with bacon or ham.

2 cups quick oats	1/4 **cup melted butter**
1/2 **cup brown sugar**	3/4 **cup milk**
1 tsp. baking powder	**1 egg**
1 tsp. cinnamon	1/2 **cup favorite nuts**
1/4 **tsp. salt**	**and dried fruits**

Mix first 5 ingredients together (oats through salt). Add butter, milk, and egg; mix well until thoroughly combined. Fold in your choice of nuts and dried fruits. Pour into greased 8 cup loaf pan. Bake at 350° for 35 minutes. Let cool for 5 minutes.

Serves 6 to 8   *Joanne Anderson Blacksburg, VA*

Stewed Cinnamon Apples

6 cups chopped and peeled
   Granny Smith apples
   (about 7 apples)
1/4 cup packed brown sugar
1/2 tsp. vanilla extract
1/4 cup apple juice

1 tsp. ground
   cinnamon
1/8 tsp. ground
   nutmeg
Dash salt

Combine all ingredients in a large heavy saucepan. Bring to a boil, then reduce heat to low. Cover and simmer for 45 minutes or until apples are tender, stirring occasionally. Serve warm.

Makes 4 cups

Hash Brown Casserole

1 large bag frozen hash
  browns, thawed
1/2 cup melted butter
1/2 cup chopped onion
1 tsp. salt
1/2 tsp. pepper

1 (10.5 oz.) can
  cream of potato
  soup
2 cups sour cream
2 cups shredded
  Cheddar cheese

Topping:
2 cups crushed corn flakes
1/4 cup melted butter

Preheat oven to 350°. In a large mixing bowl, combine all ingredients except topping. Pour into a 13 x 9 greased casserole dish. In a medium mixing bowl, mix topping ingredients. Sprinkle over the potatoes. Bake uncovered for 45 minutes.

Makes 15 generous servings

Susan Vietmeyer, class of '93
Arlington, VA

Cheese Danish

This recipe makes 2 large danishes which are then cut to make 12 to 24 slices.

2 (8 oz.) cans crescent
  roll dough
1 (8 oz.) pkg. cream
  cheese, softened
3/4 cup sugar, divided

1 tsp. vanilla extract
1 tsp. cinnamon
2 tsp. melted butter

Unroll crescent dough, pinching seams together, and cut into 4 rectangles. Place 2 rectangles on a baking sheet to make the bottom halves of each danish. Using a mixer, beat cream cheese, 1/2 cup sugar and vanilla on medium speed until smooth. Spread over the bottom halves, leaving a small border. Place remaining 2 rectangles over bottoms. Press edges to seal. Score the top of each danish with a knife at a diagonal to make 3 decorative marks. Combine remaining sugar and cinnamon. Brush dough with butter, and sprinkle with sugar mixture. Bake at 375° for 15 minutes, or until danishes are golden brown. Cool. Serve immediately, or cover and refrigerate until ready to serve. Cut into slices.

Makes 24 slices

Mini Cinnamon Rolls

The smell of fresh baked cinnamon rolls will wake you up and start your football game day right.

2 (8 oz.) cans refrigerated
   crescent rolls
6 tbsp. butter, softened
1/3 cup firmly packed
   brown sugar
1/4 cup chopped pecans
1 tbsp. sugar

1 tsp. cinnamon
1 tbsp. whole milk,
   or half and half
2/3 cups powdered
   sugar
1/2 tsp. vanilla extract
1/8 tsp. salt

Unroll crescent dough, pinching seams together. Cut into 4 rectangles. Set aside. Using an electric mixer, combine butter, brown sugar, pecans, sugar, and cinnamon. Mix well, until creamy. Spread butter mixture evenly over rectangles. Roll up each rectangle, length wise, like a jelly roll. Place rolls on baking sheet in freezer for 10 minutes. Remove from freezer. Using a serrated knife, gently cut each roll into six 1-inch slices. Place rolls, 1/4 inch apart on two 8-inch greased cake pans. Bake at 375° for 15 to 18 minutes until golden brown. Cool for 10 minutes. In a small mixing bowl, combine milk, powdered sugar, vanilla and salt. Mix well and pour over warm rolls.

Makes 24 miniature rolls

Banana Oatmeal Bread

1/4 cup butter, softened
1/2 cup sugar
2 large eggs, beaten
1 tbsp. water
4 ripe bananas, mashed
1 1/2 cups all-purpose
    flour
1/2 tsp. salt

1/2 tsp. baking soda
1/2 tsp. cinnamon
2 tsp. vanilla extract
3/4 cup old fashioned
    oats
3/4 cup finely
    chopped walnuts

Using an electric mixer, cream together butter and sugar until light and fluffy. Add eggs. In a separate bowl, combine water and mashed bananas. In another bowl, combine flour, salt, baking soda, and cinnamon. Add flour and bananas alternately to butter mixture. Mix thoroughly after each addition. Stir in vanilla, oats and walnuts. Pour into a large loaf pan. Let stand at room temperature for 30 minutes. Preheat oven to 350°. Bake for 45 to 50 minutes, or until toothpick comes out of center of bread clean. Cool for 10 minutes and remove from loaf pan.

Makes 1 loaf

Orange and Maroon Loaf

Cut this bread into slices for a proud display of Hokie colors.

2 cups all-purpose flour
3/4 cups sugar
1 tbsp. baking powder
1/2 tsp. salt
1 cup diced dried apricots
1 cup chopped fresh
  cranberries
1/2 cup coarsely chopped nuts

2 eggs
1/4 cup milk
1/4 cup melted butter
  or margarine
1 tsp. grated lemon
  rind

Combine flour, sugar, baking powder, and salt in a large bowl. Stir in apricots, cranberries, and nuts coating well. Make a well in the center of the dry ingredients. In a small bowl, beat eggs slightly; stir in milk, butter, and lemon rind. Pour into center of flour mixture; stir until dry ingredients are moistened. Pour batter into greased 9 x 5 x 3 loaf pan. Bake at 350° for 1 hour or until done. Let cool 10 minutes, remove to wire rack then cool completely.

Makes 1 loaf

Pumpkin Bread

Buy two disposable loaf pans to bake this. Bring one to the game, freeze the other one for the next game.

3 1/2 cups all-purpose flour
3 cups sugar
1/2 tsp. baking powder
2 tsp. baking soda
1 1/2 tsp. salt
1 tsp. cinnamon
1 tsp. nutmeg

1 tsp. cloves
4 eggs, beaten
2 cups canned
   pumpkin
1 cup water
1 cup oil

Combine all ingredients in a large bowl and mix well. Pour batter into two greased loaf pans. Bake at 325° for 1 1/2 hours or until toothpick comes out clean.

Makes 2 loaves

Applesauce Spice Cake

1 box spice cake mix
1 (3 oz.) pkg. instant
  vanilla pudding
4 eggs

1/2 cup water
1/3 cup canola oil
1 cup applesauce
Powdered sugar

Using an electric mixer, combine all ingredients. Set mixer on medium for 4 minutes; mix well. Pour batter into a greased Bundt pan. Bake at 350° for one hour. Cool in pan for 10 minutes. Remove from pan. Cool on wire rack completely. Before serving, sprinkle with powdered sugar.

Makes about 16 slices

Apple Date Spread

This versatile spread is great on bagels, gingersnaps, and apple slices. Serve for breakfast or dessert. Add a dash of lemon juice to chopped apples to prevent browning.

1 (8 oz.) pkg. cream cheese, softened
1 1/2 cups finely chopped pecans
1 cup finely chopped unpeeled apple

3/4 cup dried dates, finely chopped
Dash of cinnamon

Using a mixer on low speed, beat cream cheese until well blended. Stir in pecans, apple, dates and cinnamon. Chill 1 hour before serving.

Makes 2 1/2 cups

Honey and Walnut Spread

Serve this cream cheese spread on our banana or pumpkin bread.

1 (8 oz.) pkg. cream cheese, softened	1/3 cup finely chopped walnuts
1/4 cup honey	1 tsp. cinnamon

Using an electric mixer on low speed, combine ingredients and mix until well blended. Chill 1 hour before serving.

Makes 1 1/2 cups

Veggie Cream Cheese Spread

Smoked salmon is great on a bagel with this flavored cream cheese.

1 (8 oz.) pkg. cream cheese, softened
2-3 carrots, peeled and grated
6 green onions, chopped

Using an electric mixer on low speed, combine ingredients and mix until well blended. Chill 1 hour before serving.

Makes 1 1/2 cups

1ST QUARTER

APPETIZERS
&
BEVERAGES

The car is unloaded, your tailgate tent is up, and the grill is fired. Time to start this pre-game party! This chapter has everything Tech fans need to rally the Hokies to victory. From hot dips to cool spreads and cold drinks to warm brew, your fans will cheer for more. Make a big play with Running Back Dip and wait for the high-fives. Don't forget to pass around the fun-sized Mini Cheese Footballs.

Easy Mini-Pizzas

1 loaf frozen bread
  dough, thawed per
  package directions
1 (16 oz.) jar pasta sauce
1 cup shredded part-
  skim mozzarella cheese

Toppings of your
  choice
Olive oil
Cornmeal

Preheat oven to 425°. Grease two baking sheets with cooking spray. Cut bread dough into 1/2-inch thick slices. Flatten slightly and place on baking sheet, about 1 inch apart. Using a pastry brush, lightly brush slices with olive oil. Sprinkle edges with cornmeal. Spread an even amount of sauce on each pizza. Sprinkle with cheese and toppings. Bake for 15 to 20 minutes or until crusts are browned and topping is bubbly.

Makes 12 pizzas per loaf

Pepperoni and Cheese Rolls

If you like strombolis, you'll love these rolls. Feel free to add your own pizza toppings.

1 (15 oz.) package
  refrigerated pie crust
1/4 cup grated Parmesan
  cheese
1 cup shredded Cheddar
  or mozzarella cheese

1/2 lb. deli ham,
  sliced thin
1/2 lb. pepperoni,
  sliced thin
Pizza sauce

Heat oven to 450°. Bring pie crusts to room temperature. Smooth out fold lines on crusts. Leaving a 1-inch border, sprinkle each crust with Parmesan cheese; top with Cheddar cheese, ham and pepperoni. Loosely roll up each crust. Fold ends under. Place rolls, seam side down, on ungreased cookie sheet. Bake for 15 minutes or until golden brown. Cool for 10 minutes. Cut each roll into 16 slices. Serve warm with pizza sauce.

Makes 32 slices

Baked Wontons Shells

Baked wontons make an excellent shell for many types of meats, salads, and even desserts. The following two recipes are party favorites. If you're taking them to a tailgate, add the filling just before you serve them so your shells won't get soggy. Have guests "build your own".

To prepare wontons:
Purchase small wonton wrappers (usually found in the produce section of the grocery store.) Preheat oven to 350°. Lightly grease muffin pan. Place wonton wrappers in muffin pan gently pressing the center of the wrapper into the bottom of the pan to form a shell. Lightly brown in oven 8 to 10 minutes. Remove to cookie sheet. Cool

South of the End-Zone Stars

1 lb. ground beef
1 cup medium salsa
1 cup shredded Mexican style cheese
24 baked wonton shells*
*see recipe above

Prepare wonton shells and set aside. In a large skillet, brown ground beef and drain fat. Add salsa and cheese. Simmer 5 minutes. Scoop mixture into shells. Serve with sour cream and chopped green onions. Serve immediately.

Makes 24

Barbeque Stars

1 lb. ground beef,
   chipped beef or
   chicken
1/2 cup ketchup
3 tbsp. brown sugar

1 tbsp. cider vinegar
1/2 tsp. chili powder
1 cup shredded Cheddar
   cheese
24 baked wonton
   shells*

*see recipe on page 37

In a large skillet, brown ground beef and drain fat. In a small bowl, mix ketchup, sugar, vinegar, and chili powder; stir until smooth. Add to meat and mix well. Add mixture to shells and top with shredded cheese. Serve immediately.

Makes 24

Stuff the Quarterback Mushrooms

4 green onions, diced
1 (3 oz.) jar real bacon
   bits
1 (8 oz.) pkg. cream
   cheese
1/3 cup mayonnaise

24 mushroom caps,
   rinsed
1/4 cup Parmesan
   cheese
1/4 cup Italian bread
   crumbs

Mix first 4 ingredients. Spoon mixture into each mushroom cap; place in a 13 x 9 baking dish. Sprinkle with Parmesan cheese and bread crumbs. Bake at 375° for 15 minutes until golden brown.

Makes 24

Sara Willard, class of '92
Roanoke, VA

Running Back Dip

This cheesy ham dip is served in its own bread bowl. So good, Lee Suggs would be "running back" for more!

2 (16 oz.) loaves
French bread
1 (8 oz.) pkg. cream
cheese
1 (8 oz.) carton sour
cream
2 cups shredded
Cheddar cheese

1/2 cup chopped ham
1/3 cup chopped green
onion
1/3 cup chopped green
pepper
1/4 tsp. Worcestershire
sauce
Paprika

Slice off top fourth of one bread loaf. Hollow out bottom section leaving a 1-inch shell. Reserve bread top for another use. Set shell aside. Cut remaining loaf into 1 1/2-inch cubes. Place bread shell and cubes on two large baking sheets. Bake at 350° for 12 minutes or until lightly browned. In a large mixing bowl, beat cream cheese at medium speed until smooth. Add sour cream and beat until creamy. Stir in Cheddar cheese and next 4 ingredients. Spoon cheese mixture into bread shell, wrap in heavy duty aluminum foil and place on baking sheet. Bake at 350° for 30 minutes. Unwrap and place on serving platter. Sprinkle with paprika and serve with toasted breadcubes.

Makes 13 servings

Vicki Moncrief, Hokie Mom
Clarksville, TN

Onion Soufflé

3 (8 oz.) pkgs. cream cheese
1 cup grated Parmesan cheese
1/2 cup mayonnaise

1 medium onion,
minced

With an electric mixer, mix cheeses and mayonnaise. Add onion; mix well. Place in a lightly greased soufflé dish. Bake at 400° for 20 minutes. Serve with melba rounds or crackers.

Makes about 4 cups

Annie Lou Perkins, Hokie Grandmother
Gallatin, TN

Sautéed Mushrooms n' Onions

This slow cooked recipe should be made the day before to maximize the rich flavor. Reheat slowly before serving.

1/4 **cup sweet butter**	1 **tsp. salt**
11/2 **lbs. mushrooms, sliced**	1/2 **tsp. pepper**
5 **medium onions,**	1/2 **cup sour cream**
sliced thin	11/2 **tsp. paprika**

In a large saucepan, melt sweet butter on medium heat. Add mushrooms, onions, salt and pepper. Sauté for 10 minutes. Reduce heat to low and simmer uncovered for 2 hours, stirring often. Remove from heat and cool slightly. Fold in sour cream and paprika. Place mushrooms and onions in a slow cooker or chafing dish set on low. Serve with crusty French bread slices or party pumpernickel bread.

Makes 21/2 quarts

Barbara Titland, Hokie Mom
St. Petersburg, FL

Hot Artichoke Dip

1 (14 oz.) can artichoke
hearts, drained
1 cup grated Parmesan
cheese
1 (4 oz.) can chopped
green chiles, drained

1 (8 oz.) pkg. cream
cheese
1/2 cup mayonnaise
1 clove garlic,
minced

On high speed, mix all ingredients together until smooth. Spread into a baking dish. Bake at 400° for 25 minutes, or until bubbly. Serve with crackers.

Makes 4 1/2 cups
Susan Vietmeyer, class of '93
Arlington, VA

Hot Spinach-Artichoke Dip

1 (14 oz.) can artichoke
hearts, drained and
chopped
1 (10 oz.) pkg. frozen
chopped spinach,
thawed and drained
1 cup mayonnaise
1 cup Parmesan cheese

1 cup shredded
mozzarella cheese
1 (2 oz.) jar roasted
red peppers,
drained and
chopped
1 clove garlic minced

Combine all ingredients and mix well. Spoon into a lightly greased casserole dish. Bake at 350° for 20 minutes or until heated and golden. Serve with tortilla chips or your favorite crackers.

Makes 6 cups
Linda Resco, Hokie Fan
Roanoke, VA

Marinated Artichoke Dip

Marinated artichokes are at the heart of this spicy dip.

2 (8 oz.) pkgs. cream
  cheese, softened
2 (4 oz.) jars marinated
  artichoke hearts with
  liquid
1/4 cup chopped red onion

1 tsp. lemon juice
1 garlic clove,
  minced
Salt and pepper
  to taste
Dash of hot sauce

Using a mixer on medium speed, combine all ingredients. Pour into a 2-quart baking dish or large ceramic crock. Bake at 400° stirring every 10 minutes. Remove when bubbling. Serve warm with whole wheat crackers.

Makes 3 cups

Diane Hutt, Hokie Fan
Asheville, NC

Blue Cheese Bites

1 can refrigerator
  biscuits
1/2 cup butter, melted

1/2 cup crumbled
  blue cheese

Grease 9-inch pie plate. Cut biscuits in fourths and place in plate. Pour melted butter over biscuits and top with bleu cheese. Bake according to biscuit directions until brown.

Makes 32

Annie Lou Perkins, Hokie Grandmother
Gallatin, TN

Hot Pizza Dip

1 (8 oz.) pkg.
  cream cheese
1 tbsp. Italian
  seasoning
1 tbsp. garlic powder
1 cup shredded
  mozzarella cheese
1/2 cup grated Parmesan
  cheese
1 cup pasta sauce
2 tbsp. finely chopped
  green pepper
2 tbsp. finely chopped
  onion
1/4 cup chopped
  pepperoni

Preheat oven to 350°. On high speed, mix cream cheese, Italian seasoning and garlic powder until blended. Spread on bottom of a small baking dish. Combine cheeses; sprinkle half over cream cheese. Pour sauce over cheeses. Top with peppers, onions and pepperoni. Sprinkle on remaining cheese. Bake for 20 minutes, or until bubbly. Serve with toasted French bread, thinly sliced.

Makes 4 cups

Susan Vietmeyer, class of '93
Arlington, VA

Baked Brie

1/2 **cup coarsely chopped pecans**	1 **lb. Brie wedge**
1 **tbsp. butter, melted**	1/2 **cup brown sugar**

Toast pecans in butter at 300° for 10 minutes, stirring occasionally. Place Brie in a 1-quart baking dish. Cover with brown sugar and sprinkle with pecans. Bake at 350° for 10 to 15 minutes or until Brie begins to melt. Serve with wheat crackers.

Makes 24 servings

Apricot Brie

Add a touch of class to your buffet with this brie.

1 **(8 oz.) Brie wedge, top of rind removed**	1/4 **cup sliced almonds**
1/4 **cup apricot preserves**	1/3 **cup diced dried apricots**
	2 **tbsp. brown sugar**

Place Brie in 1-quart baking dish. Spread on preserves; top with almonds and apricots. Sprinkle on brown sugar. Bake at 350° for 10 to 15 minutes until Brie begins to melt. Serve with crackers.

Makes 12 to 14 servings

Hot Buttered Brie

Our family has been making this Brie for 25 years. Our game day spread is never complete without this dish.

1/2 **cup sweet butter, sliced**
1 **(8 oz.) Brie wedge, top of rind removed**

1 **cup sliced almonds, toasted lightly**

Place butter slices on bottom of 1-quart baking dish. Place Brie on butter. Sprinkle almonds on top of Brie. Bake at 350° for 10 to 15 minutes until bubbly. Serve with crusty French bread slices.

Makes 12 to 14 servings

Barbara Titland, Hokie Mom
St. Petersburg, FL

Cheesy Salsa Dip

Serve in a small to medium size slow cooker to keep this dip warm and melted until the last chip is dipped!

1 **(16 oz.) loaf Velveeta cheese**
1 **(16 oz.) jar medium salsa**

In a large saucepan, heat ingredients on medium low. Stir often, until cheese is melted and blends with salsa. Serve immediately with tortilla chips.

Makes 4 cups

Chili Cheese Dip

Of course, homemade chili is a great substitute for the canned chili.

1 (8 oz.) pkg. cream cheese, softened
1 (16 oz.) can Hormel chili with beans

1 (8 oz.) pkg. shredded Cheddar cheese

Preheat oven to 350°. In a pie plate, layer cream cheese, chili, and then top with cheese. Bake in oven for 25 to 30 minutes, until bubbly. Serve with tortilla chips.

Makes 16 to 18 servings

Green Chile-Cheese Dip

2 (4 oz.) cans chopped green chiles, undrained
1/2 cup shredded Monterey Jack cheese

1 cup grated Parmesan cheese
3/4 cup mayonnaise
1 tsp. ground cumin

Combine all ingredients. Spoon into greased 1-quart baking dish. Bake at 350° for 15 to 20 minutes, until bubbly. Serve immediately with tortilla chips.

Makes 3 cups

Deviled Eggs with a Kick

6 hard boiled eggs
1/4 cup mayonnaise
2 tbsp. minced jalapeno
   slices
1 tbsp. prepared mustard

1/4 tsp. cumin
1/8 tsp. salt
Chili powder

Peel eggs and cut in half lengthwise; remove yolks. Mash yolks in a small bowl, stir in mayonnaise and next 4 ingredients. Spoon mixture into egg white halves. Sprinkle lightly with chili powder as a garnish.

Makes 12

Spicy Deviled Eggs

1 dozen hard boiled eggs
1/2 cup mayonnaise
1 1/2 tbsp. Dijon mustard

Salt to taste
Cayenne pepper

Peel eggs and cut in half lengthwise; remove yolks. Mash yolks in a small bowl, stir in mayonnaise, mustard, salt and pepper. Spoon mixture into egg white halves. Sprinkle lightly with cayenne pepper as a garnish.

Makes 24

Quick and Easy Crab Spread

1 (8 oz.) pkg. cream
   cheese, softened
1 (8 oz.) can pasteurized
   lump crabmeat, drained

1 (12 oz.) bottle
   cocktail sauce

Place cream cheese on small serving platter. Cover with crabmeat and top with cocktail sauce. Serve with your favorite crackers.

Makes 28 appetizer servings

Italian Cheese Ball

2 (8 oz.) pkgs. cream cheese
1 envelope Italian dressing
   mix

1 cup pecans,
   chopped

Mix together cream cheese and dressing mix. Shape into a ball and roll in pecans. Serve with crackers. (We prefer Sociables brand.)

Serves 10 to 12

Tonda, wife of Ronnie Fugate, class of '92
Roanoke, VA

Pecan Spread

This spread can be served either hot from the oven, or cold. It also freezes well.

1 (8 oz.) package
cream cheese
2 tbsp. milk
1/2 cup sour cream
1 (2.5 oz.) jar sliced
dried beef, chopped
1/2 tsp. garlic salt

1/4 tsp. pepper
1/4 cup finely chopped
green pepper
2 tbsp. finely
chopped onion
1/2 cup chopped
pecans

On medium speed, mix together cream cheese and milk. Fold in sour cream. Add beef, garlic salt, pepper, green pepper and onion. Mix well, and pour into a greased 1-quart casserole dish. Top with pecans and spray lightly with vegetable oil spray. Bake at 350° for 15 minutes. Serve with crackers.

Makes 2 cups

Milan Tolley, Hokie Fan
Christiansburg, VA

Goal Line Guacamole Dip

3 ripe avocados,
  1/2 mashed,
  1/2 coarsely chopped
1 ripe tomato,
  seeded and diced
1/2 tsp. sour cream
1/2 tsp. mayonnaise

1 tsp. minced
  red onion
1/2 tsp. fresh lemon juice
1 garlic clove, minced
Salt and pepper to taste
Fresh cilantro

Combine all ingredients except cilantro in a medium mixing bowl until blended. (Be sure to keep part of the avocado chunky.) Garnish with fresh chopped cilantro. Serve with tortilla chips or fresh vegetables.

Makes about 2 cups   *Kelly Christensen, class of '92*
San Francisco, CA

Black Bean Dip

2 (15 oz.) cans black beans,
  rinsed and drained
2 cups shredded Mexican
  blend cheese
1/2 cup chopped green onions

1 cup salsa
1 tbsp. dry
  cilantro
1 1/2 tsp. cumin

Combine all ingredients; mix well. Refrigerate. Serve with tortilla chips.

Makes about 4 cups
Candace, wife of Dan Tilley, class of '90
Huntersville, NC

Layered Mexican Dip

1 1/2 cups bean dip
1 cup guacamole
1 1/2 cups sour cream
1/4 cup mayonnaise
1 tbsp. chili powder
1 tsp. cumin
2 cups shredded
  Cheddar cheese

3/4 cup diced tomatoes
1/2 cup chopped black
  olives
1/4 cup chopped sweet
  onion

Using a 9-inch pie plate, or an 8 x 8 baking dish, spread bean dip evenly on the bottom. Spread guacamole over bean dip. Set aside. In a medium sized mixing bowl combine sour cream, mayonnaise, chili powder, and cumin. Spread evenly over guacamole layer. Sprinkle cheese over layers. Top with tomatoes, olives and onions. Refrigerate 2 hours. Serve with tortilla chips.

Makes 8 cups

Inn at Riverbend Texas Caviar

3 cans black-eyed peas,
   drained and rinsed
1 red bell pepper,
   chopped

1 purple onion,
   chopped
Fresh cilantro,
   chopped

Dressing:
1/4 cup white vinegar
6 tbsp. red wine vinegar
6 tbsp. vegetable oil

6 tbsp. sugar
Cayenne pepper,
   to taste

Combine the first four ingredients in a bowl. Set aside. Combine the dressing ingredients and mix well. Pour over the pea mixture; chill. Serve with chips called "Scoops".

Lynn and Linda Hayes, Hokie Fans
Pearisburg, VA

Mexican Rollups

You can substitute roasted red peppers for the olives in this recipe.

2 (8 oz.) pkgs. cream cheese, softened

1 (6 oz.) can pitted black olives, drained and chopped

2 (4 oz.) can chopped green chiles, undrained

1/2 cup chopped red onions

8 (10 1/2-inch) flour tortillas

1 jar medium salsa

Using a mixer on medium speed, mix together cream cheese, olives, chiles, and onions. Place a large spoonful of cheese mix in the center of each tortilla. Spread evenly, and tightly roll up tortilla. Wrap tortilla in plastic wrap and refrigerate for 8 hours, or overnight. Take tortillas out of plastic. Slice each tortilla into several one inch slices and secure with a toothpick. Serve with salsa.

Makes up to 7 dozen   *Melody Thomas, class of '97*
Blacksburg, VA

Spinach Dip

This very popular dip recipe looks great in a hollowed out bread bowl.

1 (10 oz.) pkg. frozen spinach, thawed and drained thoroughly
1 cup mayonnaise
1 cup sour cream
1 (4 oz.) can sliced water chestnuts, drained and chopped
1/4 cup chopped red onion
1 pkg. vegetable soup mix

In a large bowl, combine all ingredients and mix well. Refrigerate for several hours before serving. Serve with vegetables, crackers, or bread pieces.

Makes 4 cups

Chrissy Mazur, class of '97
McLean, VA

Game-Winning Cheese Dip

1/4 cup pecans
2 strips bacon, cooked
  and crumbled
1 cup shredded sharp
  Cheddar cheese

1 tbsp. minced green
  onion,
2/3 cup mayonnaise
1/4 tsp. salt

Roast pecans at 350° for 3 to 4 minutes. Chop when cool. Mix well with remaining ingredients. Serve with buttery crackers.

Makes 2 cups

Annie Lou Perkins, Hokie Grandmother
Gallatin, TN

Mini Cheese Footballs

1 (8 oz.) pkg. cream
  cheese, softened
2 cups finely shredded
  Cheddar cheese
1 1/2 cups grated carrot

2 tbsp. honey
2 cups finely
  chopped pecans
Pretzel sticks

Using an electric mixer, combine the first four ingredients. Mix well; cover and chill 1 hour. Shape into 1 inch mini footballs and roll in pecans; cover and chill. Place a pretzel stick in each football when serving.

Makes about 4 dozen footballs

Ranch Dip

Serve in hollowed out bell peppers to add color to your table.

1 cup small curd cottage cheese	1 (1 oz.) pkg. Ranch-style dressing mix
1 cup carton sour cream	
3/4 cup mayonnaise	

In a medium bowl, combine all ingredients; mix well. Refrigerate at least one hour before serving. Serve with crackers and fresh vegetables.

Makes about 3 cups

Honey Mustard Dip

This dip is excellent for pretzels, or can accompany the Hot Ham and Cheese Rolls or Honey Pecan Chicken Tenders.

3/4 cup sour cream	1/4 cup Dijon mustard
1/4 cup mayonnaise	1 tbsp. cider vinegar
1/4 cup honey	

In a small bowl, combine all ingredients. Chill several hours before serving.

Makes about 1 1/4 cups

Seasoned Pretzels

1 cup margarine
1 envelope onion soup mix
1 box sourdough pretzels, broken
   into bite-sized pieces

Melt margarine in a large skillet; add soup mix and stir well. Add pretzels; stir to evenly coat the pieces. Transfer to cookie sheet. Bake at 250° for 2 hours, stirring often. Cool. Store in an airtight container.

Makes 7 cups   *Beverly Teske, class of '90*
                                                      Riner, VA

Seasoned Oyster Crackers

This snack tastes great with Bloody Marys or beer.

1 box oyster crackers
1 envelope Ranch dressing mix
3/4 cup Orville Redenbacher's popcorn oil

Place all ingredients in a large bowl and mix well. Let it sit for 5 minutes and stir again. Repeat. Store in an airtight container.

Makes about 6 cups   *Beverly Teske, class of '90*
                                                    Riner, VA

Snack Mix

3 cups popped popcorn
2 cups Goldfish crackers
2 cups Wheat Chex
2 cups oyster crackers
2 cups salted mixed nuts

2 cups pretzel sticks
1 envelope Ranch
  style dressing
  mix
1/3 cup melted butter

Preheat oven to 250°. In a large bowl combine first 6 ingredients. In a small bowl, mix together dressing mix and butter. Combine dressing with dry ingredients. Spread the mix on an ungreased baking sheet and bake for 15 minutes; stirring every 5 minutes. Cool completely. Store in an air tight container lined with a paper towel.

Makes approximately 12 cups

Fruited Tea

Feel free to spike this cool drink with a little rum.

4 family-sized tea bags   1 cup sugar
1 tub Crystal Light   Water
    lemonade mix   Ice
1 (46 oz.) can pineapple juice

Brew tea in 3 cups hot water; cool slightly. Pour into 1 gallon pitcher. Add next three ingredients and mix well. Add water to fill pitcher to the top. Serve over ice.

Makes 1 gallon

Hokie Bird Punch

A great punch for the little Hokies.

1 (46 oz.) can unsweetened
    pineapple juice
1 bottle cranberry juice
1 quart club soda

Combine all ingredients. Chill. Serve over ice.

Makes just over a gallon.

Beat the Hurricanes Punch

The drink of choice before the Miami game.

1 cup dark rum	1/4 cup passion fruit
1 cup light rum	syrup
1 cup apricot nectar	4 tsp. grenadine
1 cup strawberry nectar	4 tsp. lime juice

Mix well in a large pitcher with ice.

Serves 6

Yummy Margaritas

8 (6 oz.) cans limeade	3 1/2 quarts water
1 liter triple sec	1 cup bottled lime juice
1 1/2 fifths tequila	Coarse salt for glasses

Combine all ingredients in an extra large thermos. Serve over ice with salt on glass rim.

Serves many

Susan Vietmeyer, class of '93
Arlington, VA

Mimosas

1 (750 ml.) bottle Champagne or sparkling wine
1/3 cup Cointreau or triple sec
2 quarts orange juice

Gently mix ingredients just before serving.

Makes 10 cups

Strawberry Mimosas

2 1/2 cups orange juice
1 (10 oz.) pkg. frozen strawberries,
    partially thawed
1 (750 ml.) bottle Champagne or sparkling wine

Combine orange juice and frozen strawberries in blender. Process until pureed. Pour into a pitcher; add champagne and stir gently. Serve immediately.

Makes 8 cups

Bloody Marys

1 (32 oz.) can tomato
   juice
3/4 **cup vodka**
1/4 **cup lemon juice**
2 tsp. Worcestershire sauce

1/4 tsp. celery salt
Dashes hot pepper
   sauce

Stir all ingredients together in a pitcher. Serve over ice and garnish with celery stalk.

Makes about 5 servings

Southgate Sangria

1 peach, pitted
   and sliced
5 strawberries, sliced
1 orange, sliced in
   rounds

1/4 cup Cointreau*
1 bottle dry red wine,
   such as Spanish Rioja
2 tbsp. sugar
2 cups orange juice

Soak the fruit in Cointreau for at least one hour. Pour into a large pitcher with some ice. Add remaining ingredients. Mix well.

*or Grand Marnier

Serves many

Sea Breeze Punch

1 (64 oz.) bottle cranberry
  juice cocktail
1 (48 oz.) can grapefruit
  cocktail juice
2 cups vodka

2 cups seltzer
  water
2 limes, thinly
  sliced

Combine ingredients in a large container or pitcher.
Chill. Serve over ice; make sure to put a lime slice in
every glass.

Makes just over a gallon

Fuzzy Blue Gobbler

1 part Peach Schnapps
1 part Maui Blue Hawaiian Schnapps
1 part Wild Turkey brand bourbon

Combine ingredients in a large pitcher. Chill. Serve
over ice.

Hot Spiced Cider

What a great hot drink for those chilly fall tailgates.

1 gallon apple cider, or
  juice
1/2 cup brown sugar
5-6 whole cloves

8 cinnamon sticks
1 orange, thinly
  sliced

In a large stockpot simmer all ingredients on medium low heat for approximately 40 minutes. Strain spices and orange. Serve hot.

Makes 1 gallon

Warm 'n Cozy Gobbler

1 part Wild Turkey
5 parts hot apple cider

Serve hot.

Highty Tighty Hot Chocolate

3 cups milk
3/4 **cup half and half**
1/2 **cup sugar**

1/2 **cup cocoa**
1 tsp. vanilla
1/4–1/2 **cup bourbon**

Combine milk and half and half in a medium sauce pan; cook over medium heat until thoroughly heated (do not boil). Add sugar and cocoa, whisking until blended. Remove from heat, whisk in vanilla and bourbon. Pour into mugs; top with marshmallows.

Makes 41/2 cups

2ND QUARTER

SOUPS, SALADS
&
SANDWICHES

Game day temperatures can be hard to predict in Blacksburg. Whether it's a hot fall day or a cold wintry night, expect to satisfy your hungry tailgaters with recipes in this chapter. Nothing warms you up better than a bowl of Fightin' Gobbler Chili. For a lighter spread, check out our selection of turkey wraps.

Baked Potato Soup

Top this soup with crumbled bacon, shredded Cheddar cheese and sliced green onions.

1 cup butter
3 large sweet onions,
2 garlic cloves, minced
1/4 cup chopped fresh
   parsley
3 cups water

10 baking potatoes,
   peeled and cubed
2 bay leaves
1 1/2 tsp. salt
1/2 tsp. pepper
2 quarts half and half

In a large soup pot, melt butter. Add onions, garlic and parsley and sauté for 5 minutes. Add water, potatoes, bay leaves, salt and pepper. Stir to combine. Simmer, covered, stirring occasionally until potatoes are soft. Remove bay leaves. Using a potato masher or large fork, mash potato leaving some chunks. Stir in half and half. Heat on low, stirring often until soup is heated. Salt and pepper to taste, if necessary. Top as desired, or serve as is.

Makes 10 to 12 servings

Beef and Vegetable Stew

A hearty stew that will keep you warm during those bitter cold tailgates!

2 lbs. red potatoes, rinsed and chopped
6 carrots, peeled and cut into 1/4-inch slices
1 celery stalk, sliced
2 onions, coarsely chopped
2 lbs. cubed stewing beef, excess fat removed

1/2 tsp. salt
1/2 tsp. pepper
1/3 cup flour
1 (14.5 oz.) can diced tomatoes, w/ juice
1 cup beef broth
1/2 cup burgundy wine
1 tbsp. chopped fresh parsley
1-2 bay leaves

In a slow cooker, mix potatoes, carrots, celery and onion. In a large bowl, mix together salt, pepper and flour. Toss beef in flour mixture to coat; place beef and flour mixture in crock pot. In another bowl, mix together tomato, wine, broth, parsley and bay leaves. Pour into slow cooker. Cover and cook on high for 1 1/2 hours. Mix stew. Cover again, and reduce heat to low and cook an additional 6 to 7 hours, until beef is tender.

Makes 6 to 8 servings

Cuban Black Bean Soup

This is an old Moncrief family favorite from the Cuban restaurant La Zaragazona in Old San Juan. It tastes even better the next day.

1 lb. dried black
  beans, soaked
2 tbsp. salt
3 medium onions,
  minced
3 green peppers,
  minced

2/3 cup oil
2 tbsp. vinegar
1 1/2 tsp. oregano
5 cloves garlic, minced
1 1/2 tsp. cumin
2 quarts beef stock

Chopped onion
Cooked rice

Place beans and salt in a Dutch oven. Cover with water 2 inches above beans; cook until tender, set aside. Sauté onions and green peppers; add to beans. Blend together oil, vinegar, oregano, garlic, and cumin; add to beans. Add beef stock and simmer for 4 hours or until thick. Garnish with chopped onion and rice.

Makes 10 to 12 servings

Brunswick Stew for a Crowd

1 (5 lb.) chicken	3 qts. butterbeans
3 lbs. stew beef	1 gal. corn, drained
1/4 lb. bacon, chopped	1/4 stick butter
6 lbs. potatoes, diced	6 tbsp. salt
1 bunch celery	2 cups sugar
1/2 lb. carrots	1 tbsp. black pepper
1 lb. onions, diced	2-3 tbsp. Worcester-
1 1/4 gal. canned	shire sauce
diced tomatoes	1 qt. V-8 juice

Place chicken in a medium stock pot. Add just enough water to cook; bring to a boil, cover and reduce heat. Simmer for about 1 hour until chicken is cooked enough so the skin and bone can be removed. Saving the stock, remove chicken and allow to cool. Remove the skin and bone and discard; pull meat apart or coarsely chop; set aside.

In a 5 gallon stock pot, with enough water to cook, add beef and bacon. Cook until beef is tender. Add potatoes, celery, onions and stock from chicken; bring to a boil, reduce heat and simmer until potatoes are tender STIRRING AT ALL TIMES. Add chicken, tomatoes, butterbeans, and corn; bring to a boil, reduce heat and simmer. Add butter, salt, sugar, pepper, Worcestershire and V-8; cook, stirring continuously, until stew thickens. Season to taste.

Makes 5 gallons

Denny Throckmorton, Verona, VA

Cheesy Vegetarian Chili

2 tbsp. oil
2 garlic cloves,
  minced
1 bell pepper, chopped
1 sweet onion, chopped
1 cup sliced
  mushrooms
2 (15 oz.) cans diced
  tomatoes, Mexican
  style
1 (15 oz.) can tomato sauce

2 tbsp. chili powder
1 tsp. ground cumin
1/2 tsp. black pepper
2 (15 oz.) cans black
  beans, drained
1 1/2 cups diced zucchini
1 (10 oz.) pkg. frozen
  sweet corn
1 1/2 cups shredded
  Cheddar cheese

In a large saucepan, slowly heat oil and garlic on medium heat. Stir in pepper, onion, and mushrooms. Sauté for 5 minutes, until softened. Add diced tomatoes, tomato sauce, chili powder, cumin, and black pepper to vegetables. Simmer for 5 minutes. Stir in black beans, zucchini, and corn and cover. Reduce heat and simmer for 15 minutes, until bubbling. Remove from heat; slowly stir in grated cheese. Serve with sour cream and nacho chips, or over rice.

Makes 8 to 10 servings

White Lightening Chili

2 (15 oz.) cans white beans, rinsed and drained
4 (14.5 oz.) cans chicken broth
1 large onion, chopped
2 cloves garlic, minced
1 1/2 tsp. white pepper
1 tbsp. dried oregano
1 tbsp. ground cumin
1 tsp. salt
1/4 tsp. ground cloves
5 cups chopped cooked chicken
2 (4.5 oz.) cans chopped green chiles, drained
1 jalapeno pepper, finely chopped
1 1/2 cups sour cream

In a slow cooker crock pot, combine all ingredients *except* the sour cream. Mix well. Heat on low for 2 to 3 hours. Turn slow cooker off, and let chili sit for 20 minutes. Fold in sour cream and serve.

Serves a crowd

Ann Ferrell, Hokie Fan
Blacksburg, VA

Fightin' Gobbler Chili

1 1/2 lbs. ground beef
1 large onion, chopped
1 green pepper, chopped
1 tsp. salt
1 1/2 tbsp. chili powder
1/2 tsp. black pepper
1 1/2 tsp. cumin
1/4 tsp. allspice
2 (16 oz.) cans diced tomatoes
2 (15 oz.) cans red kidney beans
1 1/2 tbsp. sugar
1/2 oz. semisweet chocolate
1 (4 oz.) can tomato paste
1 (14.5 oz.) can condensed beef consommé

In a large stock pot, brown ground beef and drain. Add onion and green pepper; cook until translucent. Add remaining ingredients. Simmer several hours. Serve with grated cheese.

Serves 8 to 10

Mike Harman, class of '69
Roanoke, VA

Hokey Pokey Chili

1 lb. ground turkey
3 garlic cloves, minced
1 sweet onion, chopped
1 bell pepper, chopped
1 jalapeno pepper, no
  seeds, minced
2 tablespoons oil
3 (15 oz.) cans kidney
  beans, drained
2 (15 oz.) cans tomato sauce

2 (14.5 oz.) cans
  diced tomatoes,
  with green chiles
2 1/2 tbsp. chili
  powder
1 tsp. ground cumin
Dash hot sauce
Salt and pepper

In a large skillet, brown ground turkey and drain. Set aside. Using a large saucepan, heat jalapeno pepper, garlic and oil on medium. Add onion, bell pepper and sauté for 5 minutes. Stir in kidney beans, tomato sauce, diced tomatoes, chili powder, cumin, hot sauce, salt and pepper. Mix well, cover and simmer for 10 minutes. Fold in ground turkey, reduce heat and cover, cooking for another 20 minutes, stirring often.

Makes 8 to 10 servings

Game Day Chili

3 tbsp. olive oil
1 large onion, chopped
3 cloves garlic, minced
2 lbs. ground sirloin,
  cooked and drained
1 (28 oz.) can diced
  tomatoes, undrained
1 (15 oz.) can stewed
  tomatoes, undrained
2 (15 oz.) cans kidney
  beans, drained

1/2 green pepper,
  chopped
2 tbsp. chili powder
2 tbsp. ground cumin
1/4 tsp. cayenne
  pepper
1 tsp. oregano
2 bay leaves
Salt, to taste
Pepper, to taste

In a large stock pot, sauté onion and garlic in olive oil until translucent. Add the remaining ingredients and mix well. Simmer on medium low, covered for 2 hours; stirring frequently.

Serves 10 to 12

Susan Vietmeyer, class of '93
Arlington, VA

Buffalo Tender Salad

This tasty salad is derived from traditional hot wings.

Chicken:
1 1/2 lbs. chicken breasts
2 cloves garlic, minced
1/4 – 1/2 cup hot sauce
1 tbsp. paprika

1/4 cup melted butter
1/4 cup fresh lemon
   juice

In a mixing bowl, stir together garlic, hot sauce, paprika, butter and lemon juice. Add chicken and marinate for 6 hours to overnight. Remove chicken and grill over medium hot coals, turning once, until internal temperature reaches 170°. Set aside and let cool slightly.

Salad:
10 small new potatoes,
   boiled, cooled,
   and quartered
1 head green leaf
   lettuce
1/2 red onion, thinly
   sliced

1 fresh tomato, diced
1 stalk celery, sliced
1 carrot, sliced
1/2 cup crumbled blue
   cheese
3/4 cup favorite blue
   cheese dressing

In a large salad bowl, assemble salad ingredients. Set aside. On a cutting board, slice chicken breasts and toss into salad. Fold in Blue cheese dressing, tossing to coat.

Serves 4 to 6

Classic Rueben Salad

A salad that is hearty enough to be a main course.

1 bag salad greens
2 tomatoes, in wedges
1 1/4 cups pumpernickel
   croutons, Pepperidge
   Farms if possible
3/4 lb. deli corned beef,
   sliced and cut into
   strips

3/4 cup shredded
   Swiss cheese
1/4 cup sauerkraut,
   well drained
1/4–1/2 cup favorite
   Thousand Island
   dressing

Toss together all ingredients, adding dressing last.

Serves 4 to 6

Julie Rhudy, class of '97
Christiansburg, VA

Mediterranean Pasta Salad

For extra tenderness and flavor, marinate chicken breasts in Italian salad dressing overnight before grilling.

2 boneless skinless chicken breast halves, grilled or broiled, cut into 1/4 inch slices*

2 cups bow tie pasta, cooked and drained

1 cup quartered cherry tomatoes

1 (4 oz.) pkg. feta cheese with basil and tomato

1/4 cup chopped red onion

1/4 cup chopped sun dried tomatoes, drained

1/2 cup Caesar salad dressing

1/3 cup fresh basil leaves cut into strips

Place all ingredients in a large serving bowl and gently toss. Serve warm or chilled. *For a seafood salad substitute grilled or broiled salmon for the chicken.*

Makes 4 servings

Jolane Rutherford, Sarasota, FL

Hokie Sandwich Bites

This is a great tasting sandwich because you get to choose your favorite meats and cheeses. The number of slices is approximate. Feel free to use more or less!

1 loaf French bread
1 (8 oz.) bottle Italian
  dressing
6 slices Cheddar
  cheese

6 slices of another
  favorite cheese
12 slices of your favorite
  deli meats

Preheat oven to 400°. Cut French bread in half lengthwise. Spread Italian dressing on both halves. Place on foil-lined cookie sheet and into oven. Bake until browned. Place cheeses on bottom half of bread loaf. Place bottom half of bread back into oven until cheese *almost* melts. Remove and place deli meat on top of cheese. Place top half of bread over meat and cut into slices to share at your party.

Serves 8 to 10

Lynn Ann King, Hokie Mom
Mt. Sterling, KY

Hot Ham and Cheese Rolls

1 lb. deli ham,
    sliced thin
1 lb. Swiss cheese,
    sliced thin

2 cans crescent
    roll dough
Dijon mustard

Carefully unroll crescent dough. Divide each roll into 2 rectangles, pinching seams together. On each rectangle, place 1/4 pound ham and 1/4 pound cheese, leaving a 1-inch space around edges. Fold into thirds. Place rolls, seam side down, on ungreased cookie sheet. Fold under edges. Bake for 15 to 20 minutes at 375°, or until golden brown. Cool for 10 minutes. Slice each roll into 8 pieces. To make smaller bite size servings, cut each piece in half. Serve with Dijon mustard for dipping.

Makes at least 32

Barbara Titland, Hokie Mom
St. Petersburg, FL

Ham Delights

2 pkgs. dinner rolls
1/2 cup margarine
1 small onion, minced
2 tbsp. sugar
2 tbsp. poppy seeds

2 tbsp. prepared
mustard
1 small pkg. Swiss
cheese
1 lb. chipped ham

Slice dinner rolls in halves. Boil together margarine, onion, sugar, poppy seed and mustard. Spread boiled mixtures on both sides of bread. Lay Swiss cheese and chipped ham on bread bottom and replace tops. Cover with foil and bake at 400° for approximately 15 minutes.

Serves 8 to 10

Lynn Ann King, Hokie Mom
Mt. Sterling, KY

Touchdown Rolls

These rolls will score big points with your tailgaters!

1 stick butter
1 medium onion,
  chopped
2 tbsp. mustard
2 tbsp. Worcestershire
  sauce

1 tbsp. poppy seeds
1/2 lb. smoked ham
  diced thinly
2 pkgs. Parker
  House style rolls

Melt butter in a large pan over medium heat. Add remaining ingredients *(except rolls)*; stir until well blended. Cover and simmer 30 minutes. Bake rolls according to package directions. Remove rolls from pans. Slice open rolls and spoon in mixture. Return rolls to pans. Cover tightly with foil and refrigerate overnight. To reheat, loosen the foil, but keep covered, at 350° until hot.

Makes about 30 rolls

Sandwich for a Crowd

2 (1 lb.) loaves
Italian bread
1 (8 oz.) pkg. cream
cheese
1 cup shredded,
Cheddar cheese
3/4 cup chopped green,
onions

1/4 cup mayonnaise
1 tbsp. Worcestershire
sauce
1 lb. fully cooked ham,
thinly sliced
1 lb. roast beef, thinly
sliced
12-14 dill pickle slices

Slice bread in half lengthwise. Leaving a 1/2-inch shell, hollow out top and bottom of bread loaves. Discard removed bread. In a large bowl, combine cheeses, onions, mayonnaise, and Worcestershire sauce; spread over cut sides of bread. Layer ham and roast beef on bottom and top halves; place pickles on bottom halves. Gently press halves together. Wrap in plastic wrap and refrigerate for at least 2 hours. Cut into 11/2 inch slices.

Makes 12 to 14 servings

Linda Cobbler, Hokie Mom
Rocky Mount, VA

Turkey Cranberry Croissants

Great to make for the UVA game using Thanksgiving leftovers.

1 (8 oz.) pkg. cream
  cheese, softened
1/4 cup orange marmalade
1/2 cup chopped pecans
6 large croissants, split

Lettuce leaves
1 lb. thinly sliced
  cooked turkey
3/4 cup whole-berry
  cranberry sauce

Combine first 3 ingredients, mixing well. Spread cheese mix evenly over croissant halves. Place lettuce and turkey on croissant bottoms; spread with cranberry sauce. Cover with tops.

Makes 6 sandwiches

Pimento Cheese

For easy blending of shredded cheeses, let them sit at room temperature for 20 to 30 minutes before mixing.

1 1/2 cups mayonnaise
1 (4 oz.) jar diced
   pimento, drained
1 tbsp. finely grated
   onion
1 tsp. Worcestershire
   sauce

1 cup shredded extra-
   sharp Cheddar cheese
1 cup shredded sharp
   Cheddar
1/2 cup pickled jalapeno
   pepper slices,
   drained and chopped

Combine first four ingredients in a large bowl; stir in cheeses. Stir in chopped pepper. Serve on sliced bread.

Serves 10 to 12

Lynn Ann King, Hokie Mom
Mt. Sterling, KY

Enchilada Stacks

To make these on the grill, heat them on a griddle on low heat.

1 (16 oz.) can refried
  beans with green
  chilies
1/2 cup salsa
6 (8-inch) flour tortillas
2 cups chicken, cooked
  and chopped

2 cups chopped
  tomatoes
1 1/2 cups shredded
  Mexican blend
  cheese

In a small bowl, combine refried beans and salsa; set aside. Spray baking sheet with cooking spray. Place two tortillas on the baking sheet. Spread each with 1/3 cup refried bean mixture, then 1/3 cup chicken, then 1/3 cup tomato. Repeat layers of tortilla, bean mixture, chicken, tomato twice more. Sprinkle with 3/4 cup cheese. Bake in 350° oven for 20 minutes or until heated through. Cut into wedges and serve with sour cream.

Serves 16

Chicken Quesadillas

Make these at the game using a pan or griddle on the grill. Spray margarine is a convenient item to pack in the cooler.

8 (8-inch) tortillas
4 cups shredded
   Monterey Jack cheese
8 slices bacon, cooked
   and crumbled
4 chicken breasts,
   cooked and chopped

1 large tomato, seeded
   and chopped
3 pickled jalapeno
   peppers, chopped
3/4 cup sliced black
   olives
21/4 cups salsa

Butter one side of tortillas. Place buttered side down on an ungreased cookie sheet, set aside. Combine cheese and next 5 ingredients, and spoon mixture evenly onto 4 tortillas; top with remaining tortillas. Bake at 400° for 5 minutes, turn quesadillas and bake 5 more minutes or until cheese melts and tortillas are lightly browned. Cut into wedges and spoon salsa over each wedge.

Makes 16 to 20

Beverly Teske, class of '90
Riner, VA

Black Bean Wraps

2 (8 oz.) pkgs. cream
   cheese
2 cups shredded
   Monterey Jack cheese
   with peppers
1/2 cup sour cream
1 tsp. onion salt
2 (15 oz.) cans black
   beans, rinsed
   and drained

1/4 cup salsa
1 (10 oz.) pkg. fresh
   spinach
2 (7 oz.) jars roasted
   sweet red peppers,
   chopped
2 carrots, shredded
12 (10 1/2-inch) flour
   tortillas

Using an electric mixer blend first 4 ingredients; set aside. In a food processor or blender, process beans and salsa until smooth. Place a tortilla on a sheet of plastic wrap on a flat surface. Using a spatula, spread on a thin layer of cheese mixture; next spread bean mixture; then add a small amount of spinach, peppers and carrots. Fold two opposite sides of tortilla over slightly, then carefully roll up tortilla. Wrap tightly in plastic wrap, secure with 2 toothpicks and refrigerate. When ready to serve, cut in half and remove plastic wrap.

Makes 24

Southwestern Chicken Wraps

1 tbsp. butter
1/2 green pepper,
  chopped
1/2 medium onion,
  chopped
1 pkg. Spanish style
  rice
2 (14.5 oz.) cans diced
  tomatoes

1 lb. chicken,
  cooked, chopped
1 packet taco
  seasoning
2 cups shredded
  Mexican blend
  cheese
10-12 (10 1/2-inch) flour
  tortillas

In a medium sauce pan, melt butter over medium-high heat. Add pepper and onion; sauté five minutes. Add rice and prepare according to package directions. Once rice is tender, add tomatoes, chicken, and taco seasoning, stirring well. Place the mixture in a 13 x 9 baking dish. Bake at 350° for 20 minutes. Sprinkle with cheese and bake 5 more minutes. Serve on heated flour tortillas.

Makes about 10 wraps

Roast Beef Wraps

We recommend our own Veggie Cream Cheese on page 33 when creating these easy wraps.

2 lbs. deli roast beef, sliced thin
1 cup veggie cream cheese
6 to 8 (10½-inch) flour tortillas

Tomato slices
Green lettuce leaves
Cucumber slices

Spread a thin layer of cream cheese on a tortilla. Just below the center of the tortilla, place 2 lettuce leaves and some cherry tomatoes. Place 4 to 5 slices of roast beef on top of the lettuce and tomatoes. Leave at least 1-inch border. Fold two opposite sides of tortilla over slightly, then carefully roll up tortilla. Wrap tightly in plastic wrap, secure with 2 toothpicks and refrigerate. When ready to serve, cut in half and remove plastic wrap.

Makes 16

Turkey Curry Salad Wrap

This makes a great wrap filling with leaf lettuce. If you are in a hurry, omit the rice. You may substitute chicken for turkey

3 cups diced cooked turkey
1 1/2 cups cooked rice
1 cup chopped celery
1 cup seedless green grapes, halved
1 (4 oz.) can crushed pineapple, drained

1/2 cup chopped pecans, toasted
3/4 cup mayonnaise
1 1/2 tsp. curry powder
1/2 tsp. salt
1/4 tsp. pepper
8 (10 1/2-inch) flour tortillas

In a large mixing bowl, combine turkey, rice, celery, grapes, pineapple and pecans. In a small mixing bowl, combine mayonnaise, curry, salt and pepper. Fold into turkey mix until combined. Refrigerate for at least an hour before serving. Place a tortilla on a sheet of plastic wrap on a flat surface. Place 3/4 cup salad on the bottom half of tortilla. Fold two opposite sides of tortilla over slightly, then carefully roll up tortilla. Wrap tightly in plastic wrap, secure with 2 toothpicks and refrigerate. When ready to serve, cut in half and remove plastic wrap.

Makes 16

Classic Chicken Salad

Another excellent filling for a wrap or baked wonton.

1/2 **cup mayonnaise**
1/4 **cup sour cream**
1/4 **cup chopped fresh parsley**
1 **tsp. fresh lemon juice**
1/2 **tsp. salt**
1/4 **tsp. pepper**
3 **cups chopped cooked chicken breast**
1 **cup sliced grapes**
1/4 **cup chopped pecans**

In a medium size bowl, combine mayonnaise, sour cream, parsley, lemon juice, salt and pepper. In a large bowl, combine chicken, grapes and pecans. Fold in mayonnaise mixture; cover and chill. Serve on croissants or your favorite bread.

Makes 41/2 cups

Turkey Waldorf Salad

This salad stands on its own on a bed of lettuce or as a sandwich.

3 cups diced smoked turkey
1 Granny Smith apple, chopped
2 celery stalks, diced
1/2 cup chopped walnuts
2 tbsp. fresh chopped parsley

1/3 cup mayonnaise
1 tsp. cider vinegar
1/4 tsp. salt
1/8 tsp. pepper
1 tbsp. apple butter, optional

In a large bowl, combine turkey, apple, celery, walnuts and parsley. Set aside. In a small bowl, mix together mayonnaise, vinegar, salt, pepper and apple butter. Mix well. Fold mayonnaise mixture with turkey mixture until combined. Refrigerate 1 hour before serving.

Makes about 4 cups

HALFTIME

MEATS

The players may take a break at halftime, but we bet your team will be ready for the razzle-dazzle of one of these show stopping main dishes. Sometimes you may wish to tackle a main entrée, other times pass around a variety of appetizers. This chapter is full of delicious and flexible recipes to serve as you wish. In true Hokie style, we have included several turkey recipes such as Orange-Bourbon Turkey Legs and Blue Cheese Hokie Burgers. You will notice a few recipes using bourbon. We suggest Wild Turkey brand, of course!

Easy Delicious Meatballs

| 1 (12 oz.) jar grape jelly | 45 frozen Italian |
| 1 (12 oz.) jar chili sauce | meatballs |

In a large stock pot, heat jelly over medium heat stirring frequently until smooth. Add chili sauce mixing well. Add meatballs. Cover and cook 20 minutes or until meatballs are heated through. This can also be made in a slow cooker.

Makes 45 meatballs

Lisa Giroux, class of '89
Raleigh, NC

Pizza Burgers

A pizza inspired burger with melted mozzarella and tomato sauce as toppings. You can use either sweet or hot sausage—cook's choice!

1 lb. ground sirloin
1 lb. Italian sausage, casings removed
8 slices mozzarella cheese
1 (16 oz.) jar tomato sauce

Additional topping suggestions:
Sautéed peppers, mushrooms and onions

In a large bowl, combine sirloin and sausage until well mixed. Shape into 8 1-inch thick hamburger patties. Grill over medium hot coals, 5 minutes on each side, or until internal temperature reaches 170°. Melt mozzarella cheese on top of burger for the last minute. Remove from grill, and serve on a toasted hamburger bun with tomato sauce. Top with peppers, mushrooms and onions, if desired.

Makes at least 8 hamburgers

Blue Cheese Hokie Burgers

1 lb. ground turkey
breast
1 tbsp. white wine
Worcestershire sauce
1 egg, beaten

1/4 cup crumbled
blue cheese
2 tbsp. minced fresh
parsley
Vegetable oil spray

Combine turkey, white wine Worcestershire sauce, and egg. Shape mixture into 8 thin hamburger patties and set aside. Combine blue cheese and parsley. Place 1 tablespoon of cheese mixture in the center of 4 patties. Top with the remaining 4 patties, sealing edges well. **Before** starting the grill, coat grill rack with vegetable spray. Place patties on medium-hot grill. Cook 5 to 7 minutes on each side until done, or meat thermometer reaches 170°. Serve on hamburger buns with lettuce.

Makes 4 hamburgers

Deborah Henthorn, class of '97
Blacksburg, VA

Meatball Subs to Feed a Crowd

These taste best made a day ahead.

2 cups bread crumbs
1/2 cup freshly grated
   Parmesan cheese
2 tsp. oregano
2 tsp. basil
1/2 tsp. ground hot red
   pepper
Salt and pepper to taste

2 lbs. lean ground beef
4 cloves garlic, minced
1 small onion, minced
3 tbsp. Worcestershire
   sauce
1/4 cup milk
3 eggs

3 jars prepared pasta sauce
12 sub rolls
1/2 lb. provolone cheese, sliced

In a medium bowl, combine first 6 ingredients and set aside. In a separate bowl, crumble meat; add garlic, onion, Worcestershire, and eggs mixing with your hands. Add the breadcrumb mixture to the meat alternately with milk mixing with your hands. Shape into 48 meatballs and place onto lightly greased cookie sheets. Bake at 400° for 7 minutes; turn meatballs over and bake another 7 minutes or until done. Warm pasta sauce in a slow cooker or stockpot and add meatballs. To serve, line warm sub rolls with provolone cheese; spoon on meatballs and sauce.

Makes 12 subs

Rachel, wife of David Copenhaver, class of '94
Kingsport, TN

Burruss Hall Beef Barbecue

1-3 lbs. boneless beef
    sirloin tip roast, cut
    into large chunks
3 celery stalks, chopped
1 sweet onion, chopped
1 bell pepper, chopped
1 cup ketchup
1 (6 oz.) can tomato
    paste
1 tbsp. Worcestershire sauce

1/2 cup packed light
    brown sugar
1/4 cup cider vinegar
3 tbsp. chili powder
2 tbsp. lemon juice
2 tbsp. molasses
2 tsp. salt
1 tsp. ground mustard

Place beef in a large slow cooker. Add celery, onion and pepper. In a medium size bowl, mix together remaining ingredients. Mix well and pour over beef. Cover and cook on low for 8 hours, or until meat is tender and breaks apart. *(Note: you can skim fat from cooking juices, if necessary.)* Shred beef. Serve on Kaiser rolls with coleslaw.

Makes 10 to 12 sandwiches

Beef Brisket

This recipe leaves the roast size up to you-- whether you are feeding a few or a crowd. The amount of liquid smoke and Worcestershire sauce will depend on the size of the brisket.

1 large brisket
1 bottle liquid smoke, 1 part
1 bottle Worcestershire sauce, 2 parts
Seasoned salt, liberally
Garlic power, liberally

Pierce both sides of brisket with a fork. Rub seasoned salt and garlic powder around brisket, thoroughly covering. Pour liquid smoke and Worcestershire sauce in a heavy duty zip top bag. Add brisket. Refrigerate for 24 hours, turning occasionally. To cook, preheat oven to 300°. Place brisket, fat side down, on a roasting pan and cook for 4 to 6 hours, depending on size. Serve sliced by itself or on a sandwich roll.

Serving size varies   *Ann Ferrell, Hokie Fan*
                                              Blacksburg, VA

Grilled Beef Kabobs

1 lb. top sirloin steak
1 small bottle teriyaki
  sauce
1 garlic clove, minced
1 small sweet onion,
  finely chopped
1 pineapple, cored
  and cut into chunks

1 (8 oz.) can whole
  water chestnuts,
  drained
1 tbsp. fresh
  grated ginger
2 green onions,
  sliced

Cut steak, width-wise, into 1/4 inch strips; set aside. In a small bowl, combine 1/2 cup teriyaki sauce, minced garlic, and sweet onion. Add meat strips, and marinate at least 1 hour. Discard marinade. Using skewers, alternately thread meat strips, pineapple and water chestnuts. Grill on medium hot coals, 4 to 6 minutes, turning halfway through. Use remaining teriyaki sauce, ginger and green onions for a dipping sauce. (*Note: You can use bamboo skewers; soak skewers in water at least 1 hour to prevent burning.*)

Makes 6 to 8 skewers

Pepper Steak Slices

Serve cold using a creamy Parmesan peppercorn dressing as a dipping sauce. Also excellent on top of a salad.

3 lbs. top round, or flank steak, 11/2 inches thick
3/4 cup Italian dressing
1/4 cup red wine vinegar
1 clove garlic, minced

2 tbsp. fresh parsley, finely chopped
2 tbsp. coarse black pepper

Score steak several times on each side. Place in a heavy duty zip top bag. In a medium size bowl, mix together dressing, vinegar, garlic, parsley and pepper. Pour over steak and marinate at least 8 hours, turning occasionally. Remove steak from marinade, and discard marinade. Broil steak, 4 inches away from heat source for 10 minutes per side. Or, grill on medium hot coals for 20 minutes, turning once. Remove steak from heat and place on a platter. Cool slightly, cover and chill up to 2 days. Just before serving, slice steak thinly (flank steak should be sliced on the diagonal). Serve cold.

Makes 12 to 14 servings

Chicken Wings

What is a Hokie football party without chicken wings?
Here are three ways to prepare wings:

To prepare chicken:

Rinse chicken wings and pat them dry. Cut off and discard wing tips. Cut each wing at the joint to make 2 sections. Arrange the chicken pieces in a single layer in an ungreased baking pan. Bake at 375° for 25 minutes. Drain the fat from the pan. Pour or brush sauce (see recipes on following pages) over the partially cooked chicken in the baking pan. Bake for 10 minutes; then stir the chicken and bake 10 more minutes brushing with additional sauce if needed.

Spicy Wing Sauce

3/4 **cup butter or margarine**
1/2 **cup hot sauce**
1 **envelope dry onion soup mix**
1-3 **tsp. ground red pepper**

2 1/2 **to 3 lbs. chicken wings**

Melt butter in a small saucepan; add remaining ingredients. Prepare chicken as directed above, brushing sauce on both sides. Serve with blue cheese dressing and celery sticks.

Serves 6 to 8

Barbeque Wing Sauce

3/4 cup ketchup
1/4 cup finely
   chopped onion
2 tbsp. water
4 cloves garlic,
   minced
1 tbsp. white vinegar
1 tbsp. brown sugar

1 tbsp. Worcestershire
   sauce
1 tsp. chili powder
1/2 tsp. dry mustard
1/2 tsp. dried oregano
2 bay leaves
Dash of hot pepper
   sauce

4 lbs. chicken wings

Combine all ingredients in a medium sauce pan. Bring to a boil; reduce heat. Simmer for 2 minutes, stirring occasionally. Remove bay leaves. Cook chicken as directed on previous page brushing sauce on both sides of chicken wings as directed. Serve with blue cheese dressing and celery sticks.

Serves 6 to 8

Hula Bowl Chicken Wings

1 (8 oz.) can pineapple
 tidbits, undrained
1/2 cup chunky peanut
 butter
1/4 cup chopped green
 onions
3/4 cup white wine
 Worcestershire
 sauce

1/2 cup honey
1/2 cup soy sauce
1/4 cup orange juice
1 tbsp. minced garlic
2 tsp. sesame seeds
2 tsp. hot sauce
1 tsp. minced fresh
 ginger

3 lbs. chicken wings

Using a food processor, process all ingredients until smooth. Rinse and cut chicken wings (see page 103). Pour 21/2 cups of pineapple mixture over chicken; refrigerate the remaining mixture for later use. Cover chicken and chill for 8 hours, or overnight. Baste chicken wings often with extra pineapple mixture while cooking as directed on page 103.

Serves 6 to 8

Extra-Point Chicken

This is a spin on the usual barbecue chicken.

**6 boneless, skinless
  chicken breasts
2 cups favorite
  barbeque sauce,
12 bacon slices,
  cooked crisp**

**11/2 cups shredded
  Cheddar cheese
1 ripe tomato,
  seeded and diced
2 green onions,
  thinly sliced**

Marinate chicken breasts in 11/2 cups barbecue sauce for at least 1 hour. Grill until internal cooking temperature reaches 170°. Place on baking sheet and baste with remaining barbecue sauce. Put 2 slices of bacon and 1/4 cup shredded cheddar on each chicken breast. Top with tomato and onions. Place in the oven on broil, watching until cheese melts. Serve immediately.

Makes 6 servings

Cajun Beer-Can Chicken

Rub:

1 tbsp. light brown sugar	2 tsp. dried thyme
1 tbsp. garlic powder	2 tsp. dried oregano
1 tbsp. onion powder	2 tsp. coarsely ground pepper
1 tbsp. paprika	2 tsp. sea salt

1 whole chicken, 4 to 5 pounds
2 tsp. vegetable oil
1/2 (16 oz.) can beer (tall boy)

In a small bowl combine rub ingredients. Prepare chicken, removing giblets, neck and excess fat. Rinse the chicken inside and out using cold water. Pat dry. Brush on vegetable oil and season with rub, inside and out. Set the half full can of beer on a flat surface, and carefully slide the chicken over the top so the can fits inside the cavity. Transfer bird to grill, keeping can upright. Carefully balance bird on grill using can bottom and chicken legs. Grill on medium coals until the juices run clear - chicken breast temperature should register at 170°, about 11/4 to 11/2 hours. Wearing barbecue mitts, remove chicken and can from grill, being careful not to spill the beer—it will be very hot! Let chicken rest on beer can for 10 minutes. Remove from can, discard beer. Slice up chicken and serve.

Makes 4 to 6 servings

Honey Pecan Chicken Tenders

8 boneless, skinless
  chicken breasts
  cut into strips
1/2 tsp. salt
1/4 tsp. pepper
1/4 cup honey
2 tbsp. Dijon mustard

3/4 tsp. paprika
1/4 tsp. garlic powder
11/2 cups finely crushed
  cornflakes
1/2 cup finely chopped
  pecans

Preheat oven to 350°. Sprinkle salt and pepper over chicken strips. In a small bowl, whisk together honey, mustard, paprika and garlic powder. In a shallow dish, mix together cornflakes and pecans. Cover each chicken strip in honey mix, then dredge through cornflakes and pecans. Place on a baking sheet greased with vegetable oil spray, in a single layer 1 inch apart. Lightly coat chicken with oil spray. Bake for 15 minutes, turning once. Serve with your favorite honey mustard or barbecue sauce.

Makes 8 to 10 servings

Crunchy Ranch Chicken

6 boneless, skinless
  breasts
1/2 cup buttermilk
2 cups crushed
  corn flakes

1/4 cup grated
  Parmesan cheese
1 envelope Ranch style
  dressing mix

Place chicken breasts in an 8 x 8 baking dish, and cover with buttermilk. Let sit for 15 minutes. In a shallow dish, mix together corn flakes, Parmesan cheese and ranch dressing. Roll each chicken breast in corn flake mixture and place in a greased 13 x 9 baking dish. Bake at 375° for 20 to 25 minutes, or meat thermometer inserted into center of chicken breast reads 170°.

Makes 6 servings

Crock Pot BBQ Turkey

Serve this BBQ on toasted hamburger buns with extra sauce and coleslaw.

2 turkey tenderloins, cut into 6 pieces	**1 bell pepper, diced**
Salt and pepper	**1 (15 oz.) can black beans, rinsed**
Paprika	**1 (18 oz.) bottle barbecue sauce***
1 sweet onion, diced	

*For a traditional Carolina sauce, we recommend Sauers brand barbeque sauce.

Place tenderloin pieces on the bottom of a slow cooker. Lightly sprinkle turkey with salt, pepper and paprika. In a large mixing bowl, combine onion, pepper, beans and 1/4 cup barbecue sauce. Pour over top of turkey pieces. Cover and cook on low for 8 hours. Stir a few times towards the end. Turn off slow cooker and remove cover. Let turkey cool slightly if necessary, pour off excess liquid. Shred turkey with fork and mix well with other ingredients. Add 3/4 cup barbecue sauce; stir in additional sauce if desired.

Makes 8 sandwiches

Bourbon BBQ Turkey Dogs

1 tbsp. butter
1/4 cup minced onion
1/2 cup ketchup
1 cup currant jelly

1/3 cup bourbon
10 turkey franks,
cut into bite size
pieces

Melt butter in a medium size saucepan. Add onion and sauté until the onion is translucent. In a medium size mixing bowl, combine ketchup, jelly and bourbon. Mix well. Add to the onions and stir to combine. Add turkey franks to the sauce. Simmer on medium low heat, uncovered, until the sauce begins to glaze, about 25 minutes. Serve in a chaffing dish, with toothpicks.

Makes about 10 to 12 servings

Orange-Bourbon Turkey Legs

1 1/2 lbs. turkey legs
2 cups fresh orange
  juice
1/2 cup bourbon
1/2 cup water

1/3 cup light molasses
1/4 tsp. salt
2 oranges, thinly sliced
Fresh parsley, minced

Rinse turkey legs and pat dry; place in gallon size heavy duty zip top plastic bags. Combine orange juice, bourbon, water, molasses, salt and parsley. Mix well. Set aside 1/2 cup; refrigerate. Pour remaining marinade into plastic bags, covering turkey legs. Divide orange slices and place in bags. Marinate in refrigerator 4 to 24 hours, turning bag occasionally. Remove turkey legs from bags. ***To bake:*** Place in a broiler pan coated with cooking spray. Bake at 350° occasionally basting with reserved marinade for 1 hour, or until thermometer registers 180°. ***To grill:*** Grill the turkey legs over medium coals occasionally basting with reserved marinade until meat thermometer registers 180°, about 1 hour.

Makes about 6 legs

Bourbon and Brown Sugar Turkey

This marinade is also great with pork tenderloin or flank steak!

1/4 **cup packed dark brown sugar**	1/4 **cup soy sauce**
1/4 **cup minced green onions**	1/4 **cup Dijon mustard**
1/4 **cup bourbon or water**	1/2 **coarse black pepper**
	1/4 **tsp. Worcestershire sauce**

2 turkey tenderloins, about 1 1/2 pounds

Combine all ingredients in a gallon zip top plastic bag; add turkey tenderloins. Seal bag and marinate 4 to 24 hours. Turn bag occasionally. Remove turkey from bag, discard marinade. Place tenderloins on grill. Grill on medium for 30 minutes until done. Meat thermometer should read 170°. Remove from grill, let stand for 10 minutes. Slice diagonally and serve.

Makes 8 servings

Grilled Beer Bratwurst

For a classic Bratwurst serve with sauerkraut, peppers and onions.

10 fresh bratwurst
2 (12 oz.) bottles dark German Beer
1 clove garlic, pressed

Place bratwurst in a heavy duty foil pan on grill. Add beer and garlic. Bring to a boil. Cover with foil and simmer for 15 to 20 minutes. Uncover, remove bratwurst and split lengthwise. Grill them over medium heat until browned, 6 to 8 minutes, turning once halfway through grilling time. Serve on warm Hoagie buns, with deli mustard.

Makes 10 bratwurst

Sweet and Spicy Sausage

Serve over rice for a main dish or with toothpicks for an easy appetizer. We like DELALLO brand sauce for this recipe.

1 1/4 lbs. Italian Sausage (mild or hot)
3 cups water, divided
1 (16 oz.) jar mild sweet peppers and sauce
1 cup water

Place sausage in a large skillet with 2 cups water. Cook on medium heat for about 20 minutes, or until sausage is cooked through. Remove sausage and cut into 1/4 − 1/2 inch slices. Discard contents of pan. Return sausage to pan, add sauce and 1 cup water. Simmer 15 minutes.

Makes at least 4 servings

Hokie Smokies

1 lb. bacon
1 lb. 2-inch smoked sausages
1/4 cup brown sugar

Preheat oven to 375°. Cut bacon into thirds. Wrap each sausage with a third of a slice of bacon and secure with a toothpick. Place in a single layer on a baking dish. Sprinkle with brown sugar. Bake for 40 minutes. Serve warm.

Makes about 50

Cranberry-Orange Pork Chops

Be sure to pack some wet wipes if you make these pork chops at your tailgate.

1/2 **cup orange marmalade**	**2 tbsp. honey**
1/4 **cup whole cranberry sauce**	**2 tbsp. orange zest**
2 tbsp. cider vinegar	**2 tbsp. soy sauce**
	Dash hot pepper sauce
	12 center cut pork chops

In a small bowl, whisk together first 7 ingredients. Set aside 1/4 cup of sauce. Pour remaining sauce into a 13 x 9 baking dish. Place pork chops in the sauce, covering both sides. Marinate for 2 to 3 hours. Grill over medium hot coals, turning at least once, lightly brushing with 1/4 cup of sauce. Cook until meat thermometer reads 170°.

Makes 12

Mini Maryland Crab Cakes

1 lb. fresh lump
   crabmeat
1/2 cup fine
   breadcrumbs
1/4 cup mayonnaise
2 tsp. Old Bay seasoning

2 tbsp. chopped
   fresh parsley
1 1/2 tsp. fresh
   lemon juice

Drain crabmeat and remove any bits of shell. Combine crabmeat with remaining ingredients. Shape into mini patties, about 1 1/2 inches wide. Place on a lightly greased baking sheet. Bake at 400° for 8 to 10 minutes, or until golden. Serve with tartar sauce and shredded lettuce on dinner rolls.

Makes about 4 dozen mini sandwiches

Barbecue Shrimp

1/4 **cup butter**
1/2 **cup Italian dressing**
2 tbsp. Worcestershire
sauce
3 tbsp. barbecue sauce
3 cloves garlic, minced
1 tbsp. lemon pepper

1/2 **tsp. pepper**
2 bay leaves
2 lemons, sliced
1 large onion, sliced
3 lbs. medium-sized
fresh shrimp,
unpeeled

Melt butter. Combine all ingredients in a large roasting pan. Stir, coating the shrimp well. Bake at 400° for 15 to 20 minutes, stirring occasionally until shrimp turn pink. Remove bay leaves. Serve on a large platter with cocktail sauce.

Makes 12 servings

Shrimp in Beer

Make sure to serve with lemon wedges and crusty bread, to soak up the broth. This can also be made on the grill using a heavy duty foil roasting pan.

3 lbs. medium shrimp
   peeled and deveined
1/4 cup butter
1 garlic clove, minced
1 (12 oz.) can beer
1 tsp. parsley flakes

1/2 tsp. thyme
1/2 tsp. oregano
1/2 tsp. pepper
1/2 tsp. salt
Dash red pepper
   flakes

Melt butter in a large saucepan over medium heat. Add garlic and cook for 1 minute. Add beer; add remaining ingredients. Keep on medium heat and simmer 5 minutes. Add shrimp; cover and simmer for 1 to 2 minutes, or until shrimp turn pink. Let cool slightly, serve warm or cold with lemon wedges, cocktail sauce and crusty bread slices.

Makes about 12 servings

Turkeys Gone Wild Bourbon Glaze

A simple marinade that spices up any meat.

1 cup dark brown sugar, firmly packed
4 to 6 tbsp. bourbon
2 tbsp. low sodium soy sauce
2 tbsp. fresh lime juice
1 tbsp. freshly grated ginger
2 garlic cloves, minced
1/4 tsp. salt
1/4 tsp. pepper

Combine all ingredients. Pour into large zip top plastic bag with meat. Marinate 1 hour, or overnight, turning bag occasionally. Remove meat and discard marinade. Cook meat, as desired. Garnish with sesame seeds and diced green onions.

Makes approximately 1 1/2 cups

Flank Steak Marinade

2 tbsp. cider vinegar
5 green onions, sliced
3/4 cup vegetable oil
1/2 cup soy sauce
1 1/2 tsp. freshly grated ginger
3/4 tsp. garlic powder
3 tbsp. honey

In a large, heavy duty zip top plastic bag, combine all ingredients. Place steak in bag and marinate 4 to 24 hours. Remove steak from marinade and grill over hot coals 6 minutes on each side. Slice steak thinly on the diagonal.

Makes about 1 cup

Susan Vietmeyer, class of '93
Arlington, VA

Sesame-Ginger Marinade

A great marinade for pork tenderloin or chicken strips.
Also great as a dipping sauce.

1 cup soy sauce	1 tbsp. freshly grated
1/2 cup packed brown	ginger
sugar	6 cloves garlic, minced
1/4 tbsp. sesame oil	
2 tbsp. toasted sesame seeds	

Combine all ingredients. Cover and refrigerate 1 cup of marinade to be used later as a dipping sauce. Pour remaining cup of marinade in a plastic zip top bag with meat; seal and refrigerate overnight, turning occasionally. Remove meat before cooking and discard marinade. Cook meat and serve with dipping sauce.

Makes 2 cups

Lemon Herb Marinade

Perfect for grilling chicken or turkey.

3 cloves garlic, minced
1/2 cup olive oil
1/4 cup fresh lemon juice
2 bay leaves, crushed
1/4 cup chopped fresh
   parsley

1/4 cup balsamic
   vinegar
1/2 lemon, thinly
   sliced
2 tsp. dried thyme
2 tsp. dried rosemary

Place chicken or turkey in a large heavy duty zip top bag. Set aside. In a medium mixing bowl, mix together remaining ingredients. Pour over poultry; marinate for several hours. While marinating, turn a few times. Grill poultry over medium hot coals, breast side down for 10 minutes, until skin is lightly browned. Turn and continue grilling for about 20 minutes, until internal temperature reaches 170°.

Makes about 4 servings

3RD

QUARTER

SIDES

Game-winning plays are often called from the sidelines. The tasty side dishes found in this chapter have a sneaky way of scoring big as well. Whether you're serving simple sandwiches or a roast for 20 tailgaters, they always complement the meal. In this chapter you will find traditional recipes as well as unique dishes to add variety and spice to your party. Show your school spirit with the Orange and Maroon Salad or grill it up with Hokie Packs.

Cucumber Salad

This is a fresh alternative to hamburger pickles. Garden cucumbers taste best.

3 medium cucumbers,
   peeled and sliced thin
1/4 cup cider vinegar
2 tbsp. sugar
1 tsp. dried dill weed

1/2 tsp. salt
1/2 tsp. dry
   mustard
Pepper to taste

Place cucumbers in a large salad bowl. In a small bowl, whisk together vinegar, sugar, dill weed, salt, and mustard. Pour over cucumbers. Toss well, pepper to taste. Can be served right away, or refrigerated.

Makes approximately 21/2 cups

Calico Coleslaw

1/2 head red cabbage,
   cored and shredded
2 large carrots,
   shredded
1 green pepper, cut
   into thin strips
1 yellow pepper,
   cut into thin strips
2 green onions,
   chopped

1 orange
1/4 cup rice wine
   vinegar
1 1/2 tbsp. vegetable oil
1 tbsp. honey
1 tbsp. fresh
   chopped cilantro
1/2 tsp. salt

In a large bowl, combine cabbage, carrot, peppers and onions; set aside. For dressing, zest orange peel to measure 1 teaspoon. Juice orange to yield 2 tablespoons juice. In a small bowl, whisk together zest, juice, oil, honey, cilantro and salt. Toss dressing with cabbage mix. Refrigerate at least one hour.

Makes 4 1/2 cups

Chrissy Mazur, class of '97
McLean, VA

Coleslaw Salad

Your traditional coleslaw, simple to make and easy to travel with.

1 (16 oz.) pkg. cabbage and carrot mix
1/4 head red cabbage, shredded
1 cup Marzetti's slaw dressing
1/4 tsp. pepper

Toss together all ingredients. Refrigerate at least 2 hours and up to 24 hours before serving. Store in an airtight container.

Makes about 6 1/2 cups

Orange and Maroon Spinach Salad

1 (12 oz.) can mandarin oranges, drained
1 pkg. ready to eat baby spinach
2 (15 oz.) cans whole beets drained and chopped
1/4 red onion, thinly sliced
1/2 cup coarsely chopped walnuts
1/2 cup crumbled blue cheese or goat cheese
Raspberry vinaigrette dressing

Toss together oranges, spinach, beets, onion, walnuts and cheese. Drizzle lightly with salad dressing.

Makes 8 small salads

Broccoli Salad

1 (3 oz.) pkg. cream
   cheese, softened
2 tbsp. lemon juice
2 tbsp. sugar
1/4 cup Egg Beaters
2 tbsp. vegetable oil
1 tbsp. dry mustard

1/4 tsp. salt
1/8 tsp. garlic powder
6 cups fresh broccoli
   florets
1/3 cup golden raisins
2 tbsp. chopped red
   onion

In a blender, mix together first 9 ingredients (cream cheese through garlic powder) until well blended. Set aside. In a large salad bowl, combine broccoli, raisins and red onion. Pour cream cheese dressing over broccoli and toss. Refrigerate 1 hour before serving.

Makes 12 to 14 servings

Barbara Titland, Hokie Mom
St. Petersburg, FL

Pasta with Spinach and Beans

4 cups hot cooked spiral shaped pasta	1 (19 oz.) can white beans, drained
1 pkg. ready to eat baby spinach	2 garlic cloves, minced
1/4 cup olive oil	3/4 cup grated Parmesan cheese
1/4 tsp. salt	
1/4 tsp. pepper	

In a large bowl, mix together hot pasta, spinach, olive oil, salt and pepper until spinach begins to wilt. Fold in white beans, garlic and Parmesan cheese. Serve warm or cold.

Makes 8 to 12 servings

Tortellini Salad

2 (14 oz.) pkgs. frozen
   cheese tortellini
1 green bell pepper,
   chopped
1 red bell pepper,
   chopped
1/4 cup chopped black
   olives

1 cucumber, chopped
1 (14 oz.) can artichoke
   hearts, rinsed and
   drained
1 (8 oz.) bottle Caesar
   salad dressing

Cook tortellini according to package directions. Rinse with cold water and drain. Combine with peppers, olives, cucumber, artichoke hearts and salad dressing. Mix well and refrigerate for at least 2 hours before serving.

Makes 12 to 14 servings

Green Bean Salad

1 (16 oz.) can cut
   green beans
1/2 cup vinegar
1/2 cup salad oil

2 tbsp. sugar
2 tsp. garlic salt
11/2 tsp. oregano
1 tsp. pepper

Drain beans and set aside. In a large bowl combine all other ingredients and whisk. Add beans stirring gently. Chill 1 hour. Stir before serving.

Makes 6 servings

Traditional Potato Salad

6 large potatoes
1/2 celery stalk,
   finely chopped
1/4 cup sugar
1 cup mayonnaise
1 tsp. salt

1 small onion, diced
1 whole sweet pimento,
   diced
1 tsp. pepper
1/3 cup mustard
1 cup sweet relish

Peel and dice potatoes; cook until tender. Drain, rinse with cold water and drain again. In a large bowl toss potatoes with remaining ingredients, stirring gently. Refrigerate.

Serves 8

Relish Vegetable Salad

This salad needs to be made at least 24 hours ahead. Store in an airtight container to keep fresh.

Veggies:

1 (15 oz.) can French style green beans, drained

1 (15 oz.) can corn, drained

1 (15 oz.) can small peas, drained

3 stalks celery, diced

1 medium onion, diced

1 green pepper, diced

1 (2 oz.) can diced pimiento, drained

In a large bowl, combine the vegetables. Set aside.

Dressing:

1 cup sugar

3/4 cup cider vinegar

1/2 cup vegetable oil

1 tbsp. water

1 tsp. salt

1 tsp. pepper

In a medium size mixing bowl, whisk together ingredients until sugar is dissolved. Mix with vegetables and chill in airtight container. Refrigerate 24 hours.

Makes 14 to 16 servings

Ann Ferrell, Hokie Fan
Blacksburg, VA

Marinated Vegetable Salad

A great recipe to use when summer vegetables are still in season.

Veggies:
2 cups cauliflower
   flowerets
2 cups broccoli
   flowerets
2 cups baby carrots
2 tomatoes, seeded and
   cut into thin wedges

1 red onion,
   sliced and separated
1 small zucchini,
   thinly sliced
1 small yellow
   squash, thinly sliced

In a large bowl, toss together vegetables. Set aside.

Marinade:
3/4 cup red wine vinegar
1/2 cup vegetable oil
3 tbsp. sugar

1 tsp. dried basil
1 tsp. salt
1/2 tsp. pepper

In a small mixing bowl, whisk together marinade ingredients. Pour over vegetables, toss to coat. Cover and chill at least 8 hours before serving.

Makes 12 servings

Three Bean Hot Dish

4 slices bacon	3 tbsp. cider vinegar
1 (16 oz.) can pork and beans	1/2 cup ketchup
	3/4 cup brown sugar
1 (16 oz.) can kidney beans	2 medium onions, chopped
1 pkg. frozen baby lima beans, cooked until almost tender	1 tsp. dry mustard
	2 cloves garlic, minced
	1/4 tsp. black pepper

In a large skillet, brown bacon, set aside. Sauté onion and garlic in remaining bacon grease until tender. Drain kidney and lima beans. Place in a large bowl with pork and beans; add onion, garlic and remaining ingredients. Mix thoroughly. Place in 13 x 9 baking dish and bake at 350° for 1 hour and 15 minutes. Garnish with bacon slices.

Makes 16 servings

Vicki Moncrief, Hokie Mom
Clarksville, TN

Irene's Beans

1/2 lb. bacon	3/4 cup packed brown
1 large onion, chopped	sugar
1 (15 oz.) can pork and	1 cup ketchup
beans	11/2 tbsp. light
1 (15 oz.) can lima beans	molasses
1 (15 oz.) can kidney	11/2 cups cubed
beans	Cheddar cheese

In a large Dutch oven, cook bacon, pat dry and chop coarsely; set aside reserving drippings. Using a colander, drain kidney and lima beans; set aside. In same Dutch oven, sauté chopped onion in 1 teaspoon of bacon drippings on medium for 2-3 minutes. Add bacon, beans, brown sugar ketchup, and molasses. Mix well. Fold in Cheddar cheese cubes. Cover and place dish in oven at 325°. Bake for 11/2 hours.

Makes 16 servings   *Irene Klingenberg, Hokie Fan*
Palm Coast, FL

Sweet and Spicy Beans

1 (15 oz.) can kidney beans, rinsed and drained

1 (15 oz.) can whole kernel corn, rinsed and drained

1 (15 oz.) can black beans, rinsed and drained

1 (15 oz.) can black eyed peas, rinsed and drained

1 (2 oz.) jar diced pimentos, drained

4 green onions, sliced

1/4 cup sugar

1/4 cup red wine vinegar

1/2 cup vegetable oil

1/2 tsp. ground red pepper

1/2 tsp. salt

In a large bowl, combine kidney beans, corn, black beans, black eyed peas, pimentos and green onions. Set aside. In a medium bowl, whisk together sugar, vinegar, oil, pepper and salt. Pour vinegar mixture over bean mixture; toss to coat. Cover and chill at least 2 hours, or up to 24 hours. Serve with a slotted spoon.

Makes 8 to 10 servings

Irene Klingenberg, Hokie Fan
Palm Coast, FL

Old Bay Steak Fries

2 tbsp. vegetable oil
3 large baking potatoes,
   cut in half, then into
   wedges
1 tbsp. Old Bay seasoning

1/4 tsp. pepper
Malt vinegar
Sea salt

Preheat oven to 400°. In a large bowl, mix together oil, potatoes, Old Bay and pepper. Pour onto a baking sheet. Bake for 40 minutes, or until fries are tender and crispy. To serve, sprinkle lightly with malt vinegar and sea salt.

Makes about 6 servings

Hokie Packs

These packets can be made several hours ahead, packed in a cooler ready to go to the tailgate.

4 slices bacon cooked and crumbled
4 tbsp. unsalted butter
2 oranges, sliced thick
2 red onions, peeled and quartered

3 cups large diced squash
3 tbsp. chopped fresh parsley
Salt and pepper

Place 4 sheets of 18-inch heavy duty aluminum foil, shiny side down. Place 1 tablespoon butter in the center of the bottom half of each sheet. Layer squash, onions, and oranges over butter; dividing evenly. Top each with bacon, parsley, salt and pepper. Fold top half of sheet over vegetables and bring edges together; fold each side over several times to make a tight seal. Grill on medium-high heat for 20 minutes or until squash is tender.

Makes 4 to 6 servings

Hobo Pack

Just like Hokie Packs, but this time, you choose the ingredients.

Pick a combo of vegetables - 2 cups per pack
(Potatoes, carrots, mushrooms, onions, spinach,
corn, peppers, zucchini, squash, sweet potatoes)
2 tbsp. butter per pack
Chopped parsley, garlic, and other herbs
Salt and pepper, to taste

Place a sheet of 18-inch heavy duty aluminum foil, shiny side down. Place 1 tablespoon of butter, in the center of the bottom half of the sheet. Arrange vegetables in a mound. Top with herbs of choice, salt, pepper and 1 tablespoon of butter. Fold top half of sheet over vegetables and bring edges together. Fold each side over several times to make a tight seal. Grill on medium-high heat 10 to 15 minutes or until vegetables are tender.

Makes as many as you want

Deb Henthorn, class of '97
Blacksburg, VA

Grilled Herb and Garlic Potatoes

This is a versatile potato dish that can be grilled on a barbecue, or roasted in the oven.

1 1/2 **lbs. red potatoes, scrubbed**
4 garlic cloves, unpeeled
2 tbsp. olive oil

1/2 **tsp. salt**
4 sprigs fresh rosemary,
or 1 tsp. dried rosemary
1/4 **tsp. pepper**

Cut potatoes into wedges. In a mixing bowl, combine potato wedges, garlic cloves, oil, salt, rosemary and pepper. Toss until potatoes are well coated. Spoon mixture into a heavy duty foil tray, keeping potatoes in a single layer. ***To grill:*** Grill potatoes over medium hot coals, covered with foil for 25 to 30 minutes or until potatoes are tender and crispy brown. ***To roast:*** Roast potatoes in a 450° oven, stirring occasionally for 35 to 40 minutes or until potatoes are tender and crispy brown.

Makes 4 to 6 servings

Herbed Mashed Potatoes

1 pkg. frozen mashed
   potatoes
1 (4 oz.) container herb
   cheese spread

1/4 cup butter
1 tsp. salt
1/2 tsp. pepper

Prepare potatoes according to package directions. Set aside. Using an electric mixer, whip together cheese spread, butter, salt and pepper. Fold in mashed potatoes. Pour into a greased 13 x 9 casserole dish. Spread evenly and bake at 350° for 15 minutes until lightly browned.

Makes 15 servings

Twice Baked Potatoes

These potatoes can be prepared the night before the game. Bake for the second time on game day in the oven and transport in an insulated cooler to keep warm. Or, if you're grilling, bake them at the game.

4 medium baking potatoes, baked
1/2 cup sour cream
1/2 cup shredded Cheddar cheese

1/2 tsp. garlic salt
1/4 tsp. pepper

Cut a lengthwise slice from the top of each baked potato. Discard skin from slice and place pulp in a bowl. Carefully scoop out each potato, leaving a thin shell. Beat potato pulp with an electric mixer on low speed. Add remaining ingredients and beat until smooth. Spoon mixture back into potato shells. Wrap potatoes in heavy duty aluminum foil leaving the top open. Bake at 425° for 20 to 25 minutes or until lightly browned.

Makes 4 potatoes

4TH QUARTER

DESSERTS

It's late in the game and time to bring on the unbeatable desserts found in this chapter. Then again, why wait until the 4ᵗʰ Quarter to enjoy these delicious treats? From Tech Toffee to Goal Line Brownies, victory is sweet and satisfying.

Chocolate Chip Cheese Ball

The cheese ball only holds its form if you use real butter.

1 (8 oz.) pkg. cream cheese, softened	1/4 tsp. vanilla extract
1/2 cup butter, softened	3/4 cup mini semisweet chocolate chips
3/4 cup confectioners sugar	3/4 cup chopped pecans
2 tbsp. brown sugar	

In a mixing bowl, beat cream cheese and butter until fluffy. Gradually add sugars and vanilla; beat until just combined. Stir in chocolate chips. Cover and refrigerate for 2 hours. Place chilled mixture on a large piece of plastic wrap, shape into a ball. Cover with plastic wrap and refrigerate an additional hour. Just before serving, roll cheese ball in pecans. Serve with graham cracker sticks and/or chocolate vanilla wafers.

Kim Bond, class of '90
Charlotte, NC

Fruit Kabobs with Caramel

1 (8 oz.) container cream cheese, soft style	3 large bananas, cut into 1 1/2 inch chunks
1/2 cup caramel ice cream topping	2 large Granny Smith apples, cut into large chunks
1/2 cup chopped pecans	3 cups pineapple chunks
1 1/2 tbsp. milk	

In a small saucepan, combine cream cheese and caramel ice cream topping. Cook; stirring until melted. Stir in pecans; add milk to thin sauce. Remove from heat and set aside. Alternately thread skewers with pineapple, apple and banana *(note: thread banana through the side, not the center)*. Grill for 6 minutes until heated through, turning once. Brush with caramel sauce and grill for one more minute. Cool slightly. Dip fruit in remaining caramel sauce.

Makes 8

Deborah Henthorn, class of '97
Blacksburg, VA

Pumpkin Pie Dip

We serve this at our October tailgates. For a festive touch, hollow out a small pumpkin and fill with dip.

1 (8 oz.) pkg. cream
  cheese, softened
2 cups powdered sugar
1 (15 oz.) can pumpkin
  pie filling

1 tsp. ground
  cinnamon
1/2 tsp. ground ginger

Beat cream cheese and sugar at medium speed until smooth. Add pie filling, cinnamon, and ginger, beating well. Cover and chill overnight. Garnish by sprinkling ground cinnamon over the top. Serve with gingersnaps and apple slices.

Makes about 41/2 cups

Chocolate Surprise Cookies

1 cup butter, softened	1/4 cup cocoa
2/3 cup sugar	36-48 chocolate candy
2 tsp. vanilla extract	kisses, unwrapped
2 cups all-purpose flour	3/4 cup powdered sugar

Preheat oven to 350°. In an electric mixer, cream together butter, sugar and vanilla until light and fluffy. In a medium bowl, combine flour and cocoa. Gradually add to butter mixture until well blended. Mold spoonfuls of the dough around each chocolate kiss, covering candy completely, and place on an ungreased cookie sheet. Bake 8 to 10 minutes (*note: cookies will stay in the shape of a ball*). Remove from cookie sheet and cool on a wire rack. Roll in powdered sugar.

Makes about 4 dozen cookies

Crescent School Cookies

A delicious twist on traditional crescent cookies -- without the hard work!

Dough:

2 cups butter	**1 tsp. vanilla**
1 1/4 cup powdered sugar, sifted	**4 cups all-purpose flour**

With an electric mixer, beat butter, sugar, and vanilla. Gradually add flour to form dough. Flatten and spread on a 12 x 18 cookie sheet to the edges. Bake at 350° 10 to 15 minutes just until it turns brown. Ice while warm. When completely cooled, cut into squares.

Icing:

3 cups powdered sugar, sifted	**1 tsp. vanilla**
2 tbsp. cocoa	**6 tbsp. milk**

Mix first three ingredients. Gradually add milk mixing well.

Makes 50 squares

Vicki Moncrief, Hokie Mom
Clarksville, TN

Tech Toffee Bites

50 unsalted saltine	1 (12 oz.) pkg. semisweet
crackers	chocolate chips
1 cup brown sugar	1 cup chopped pecans
1 cup butter	

Preheat oven to 400°. Line a cookie sheet with foil. Place crackers on the foil, covering the entire surface of the pan. On medium-high heat, melt butter in a sauce pan. Immediately add sugar and bring to a boil; stir constantly until slightly thickened. Carefully pour mixture over crackers. Place in oven for 7 minutes. Remove from oven and sprinkle with chocolate chips. Wait one minute, and then spread the chocolate to cover the entire surface. Sprinkle with nuts. Freeze overnight. Break into random sizes and serve.

Makes about 50 pieces
Vicki Moncrief, Hokie Mom
Clarksville, TN

Iron Hokie Chocolate Bars

13/4 cups all-purpose
    flour
1 cup sugar
1/4 cup cocoa
1/2 cup cold margarine
    or butter
1 egg, beaten

1 (14 oz.) can sweetened
    condensed milk
2 cups semisweet
    chocolate chips,
    divided
1 cup chopped nuts

Preheat oven to 350°. Mix flour, sugar, and cocoa; cut in margarine until crumbly. Add egg; mix until well blended. Reserve 11/2 cups crumb mixture. Press remaining mixture evenly on bottom of greased 13 x 9 baking pan. Bake 10 minutes. In saucepan, mix condensed milk and 1 cup chocolate chips. Over low heat, cook until chips melt and mixture is smooth. Spread evenly over first layer. Add nuts and remaining chocolate chips to reserved crumb mixture; sprinkle evenly over the top. Bake 25 to 30 minutes or until center is set. Cool. Cut into bars.

Makes 24 to 36

Goal Line Brownies

No substitutions for the butter. You've got to use the real thing!

Batter:

4 oz. unsweetened
  chocolate
3/4 cup butter
2 cups sugar

3 eggs
1 tsp. vanilla extract
1 cup all-purpose flour
1 cup chopped walnuts

Topping:

1 cup semisweet
  chocolate chips
1/4 cup water

2 tbsp. butter
1 cup whipping cream,
  whipped

In a microwave or double boiler, melt chocolate and butter; cool 10 minutes. Add sugar; mix well. Stir in eggs and vanilla. Add flour; mix well. Stir in walnuts. Line a 13 x 9 baking pan with foil and grease. Pour batter into pan. Bake at 350° for 25 to 30 minutes or until a toothpick inserted in the center comes out with moist crumbs (do not over bake). Cool completely. For topping, melt chocolate chips, water and butter in a microwave or double boiler; stir until smooth. Cool to room temperature. Fold in whipped cream. Spread over brownies. Chill before cutting. Store in refrigerator.

Makes 36

Linda Cobbler, Hokie Mom
Rocky Mount, VA

Layered Lunch Pail Bars

1 1/2 cups graham
    cracker crumbs
1/4 cup cocoa
1/4 cup sugar
1/4 cup margarine or
    butter, melted
1 (14 oz.) can sweetened
    condensed milk

2 cups semisweet
    chocolate chips
1 cup butterscotch or
    peanut butter chips
1 1/4 cups flaked coconut
1 cup chopped nuts

Preheat oven to 350° (325° for glass dish). Combine graham cracker crumbs, cocoa, sugar, and margarine. Press evenly into bottom of 13 x 9 baking pan. Pour condensed milk over crust. Layer remaining ingredients in order as listed; press down firmly. Bake 25 to 30 minutes or until lightly browned. Cool. Cut into bars.

Makes 24 to 36

Nana's Peppermint Brownies

These family recipe brownies have three layers, the brownie, a delicious peppermint candy layer, and a rich chocolate frosting.

Brownies:

1 cup butter

4 large eggs

2 cups sugar

1 1/2 cups sifted flour

2 tsp. vanilla extract

6 tbsp. cocoa

Pinch of salt

1/2 cup chopped nuts

Preheat oven to 350°. Melt butter in saucepan. Add cocoa and sugar; stir until completely blended. Using an electric mixer, beat eggs; add butter-cocoa mixture and blend. Add salt, vanilla and flour. Mix until blended. Fold in nuts. Pour into a greased 13 x 9 pan. Bake for 30 minutes, or until toothpick inserted in center comes out clean. Remove from oven and cool completely.

Peppermint layer:

1/2 cup butter, softened

1 lb. powdered sugar

1 tsp. vanilla

6 tbsp. heavy cream

1 (5 oz.) pkg. peppermint candies, finely crushed

In a large mixing bowl, beat topping ingredients until consistency is easy to spread. Spread over cooled brownies.

Chocolate frosting:

1/2 cup butter
6 tbsp. cocoa
1/2 cup heavy cream

1 lb. powdered sugar
2 tsp. vanilla

Melt butter in saucepan. Add cocoa and cream and cook over medium until it begins to thicken, about 1 minute. Remove from heat. Using an electric mixer, on low add powdered sugar to chocolate mixture one cup at a time until smooth. Add vanilla. Spread over peppermint frosting. Let brownies set for a half hour.

Makes 24 brownies

Robert Metz's Grandmother and Hokie Fan
Blacksburg, VA

Pecan Pie Bars

Crust:
2/3 **cup powdered sugar**
2 **cups all-purpose flour**
1 **cup butter**

Preheat oven to 350°. Sift together sugar and flour. Cut in butter. Mix with fingers until all butter is blended; will be crumbly. Pat into a 15 x 10 pan. Bake crust about 20 minutes, until light brown.

Topping:

2/3 **cup melted butter**	1/2 **cup packed brown**
1/2 **cup honey**	**sugar**
3 **tbsp. heavy cream**	3 1/2 **cups pecans**

While crust is baking mix butter, honey, cream and brown sugar together. When well blended, fold in pecans. Set aside. When crust is baked, remove from oven and spread topping over cooked crust. Bake 25 more minutes. Remove from oven and cool. Cut into squares.

Makes about 4 dozen   *Debbie Ewing, Hokie Fan*
Blacksburg, VA

Raspberry Almond Bars

This recipe can be doubled and freezes well.

1 cup all-purpose flour	**1/2 tsp. almond extract**
3/4 cup quick cooking oats	**1/2 cup seedless raspberry jam**
1/2 cup sugar	**1/3 cup sliced almonds**
1/2 cup butter	

Preheat oven to 350°. Line an 8 x 8 pan with foil and lightly grease. Set aside. In a medium mixing bowl, combine flour, oats, and sugar. Add margarine and mix until it looks like coarse crumbs. Stir in almond extract. Press half the oat mixture evenly over the bottom of the pan; adding more, if needed, to cover bottom. Heat jam in microwave for 30 seconds on high. Pour over the oat mixture in the pan. Combine almonds and remaining oat mix, and sprinkle over jam. Bake for 25 minutes, or until edges are lightly browned. Let cool completely before removing foil from pan. Cut into bars.

Makes 12 bars

Milan Tolley, Hokie Fan
Christiansburg, VA

Caramel Oatmeal Bars

1 cup all-purpose flour	1 cup semisweet
1 cup quick-cooking oats	chocolate chips
3/4 cup brown sugar,	1/2 chopped pecans
firmly packed	3 tbsp. all-purpose
1/4 tsp. salt	flour
1/2 tsp. baking soda	3/4 cup caramel
3/4 cup butter, melted	topping

Preheat oven to 350°. In a large mixing bowl, combine first 6 ingredients. Mix on low speed to form crumbs. Press half of mixture in the bottom of a 13 x 9 pan. Bake 10 minutes. Remove from oven and sprinkle with chocolate chips and pecans. In a small bowl, mix 3 tbsp. flour and caramel topping. Drizzle over chips and nuts. Sprinkle remaining crumb mixture over caramel and bake 15 to 20 minutes until golden brown. Cool. Cover and chill 1 to 2 hours. Cut into bars.

Makes 20 bars

Chocolate Chip Cheesecake Bars

1 roll refrigerated chocolate chip cookie dough	1 egg
1 (8 oz.) pkg. cream cheese, softened	1/2 cup sugar
	1/2 tsp. vanilla extract

Cut cookie dough roll in half. Press half of the dough in the bottom of an 8 x 8 pan. Using an electric mixer, mix together cream cheese, egg, sugar, and vanilla until smooth. Spread over dough in pan. Thinly slice remaining cookie dough, and completely cover cheese mix with dough. Bake at 350° for 25 minutes, until top is lightly browned. Let cool completely before cutting into squares.

Makes 12 bars

Wonton Dessert Stars

Baked wontons make a great dessert shell (see how to prepare shells on page 37). You can create a "make your own" bar with different filling and topping combinations.

Pudding Filling:
1 (3.5 oz.) pkg. instant pudding (any flavor)
1 cup milk
1 cup whipped cream or frozen whipped topping
2 tsp. vanilla extract
2 tbsp. Kahlua or Grand Marnier (optional*)*

Using an electric mixer. blend pudding mix, milk, and vanilla. When pudding begins to thicken, fold in whipped topping. Refrigerate.

Cream Cheese Filling:
1 (8 oz.) pkg. cream cheese, softened
1/4 cup sugar
2 tsp. vanilla extract
4 tsp. milk

Using an electric mixer, blend ingredients together until smooth. Refrigerate.

Toppings:
Chocolate chips
Candy sprinkles
Fresh berries
Mandarin oranges and shredded coconut

Bourbon-Chocolate Pecan Bites

These bite-sized pecan pies really hit the spot!

15-18 mini pie shells*	1/4 cup bourbon
1 1/2 cups chopped pecans	4 large eggs
1 cup semisweet mini	2 tsp. cornmeal
chocolate morsels	1/2 tsp. salt
1/2 cup sugar	1/4 cup butter, melted
1/2 cup light brown sugar	
1 cup dark corn syrup	

*Note: you can use mini phyllo shells or make your own mini shells by rolling out a pie pastry and cutting into 2 1/2 inch circles. Place in a mini muffin tin and prick with a fork. Bake at 350° for 12-14 minutes. One pie crust makes about 18 mini shells.

Sprinkle chopped pecans and chocolate morsels into each mini pie shell and set aside. Combine sugars, corn syrup, and bourbon in a large saucepan; bring to a boil over medium heat. Cook 3 minutes, **stirring constantly**. Whisk together eggs and remaining ingredients. Gradually stir about one-fourth hot mixture into egg mixture; then add to remaining hot mixture, stirring constantly. Carefully pour filling into piecrusts. Bake at 350° for about 10 minutes or until set.

Makes 15 to 18

Peach Bowl Crisp

Fruit crisps are easy to make and always a crowd pleaser. Serve with fresh whipped cream or vanilla ice cream.

2 frozen bags
  unsweetened peach
  slices, thawed
3 tbsp. sugar
1/2 tsp. vanilla extract
1/4 tsp. cinnamon
1/4 cup old-fashioned
  oats

1/4 cup all-purpose
  flour
1/2 cup packed light
  brown sugar
1/4 tsp. nutmeg
1 tsp. cinnamon
1/4 cup butter
1/4 cup chopped pecans

Preheat oven to 375°. Cut peach slices in half and place in an 8 x 8 baking dish. Stir in sugar, vanilla and cinnamon; mix well. Set aside. In a medium bowl, combine oats, flour, brown sugar, nutmeg and cinnamon. Using a pastry cutter or large fork cut the butter into the oat mixture until it turns crumbly. Sprinkle evenly on top of peaches. Bake for 35 minutes until topping is golden brown.

Makes 12 servings

Black Bottom Cupcakes

Cream cheese filling:

1 (8 oz.) pkg. cream cheese, softened
1/3 cup sugar
1 egg
1/8 tsp. salt

Dash vanilla extract
1 (6 oz.) pkg. semi-sweet chocolate pieces

Using an electric mixer, beat together cream cheese, sugar, egg, salt and vanilla until well blended. Fold in chocolate pieces. Set aside.

Cupcake bottoms:

3 cups all-purpose flour
2 cups sugar
1/2 cup cocoa
1 tsp. salt
1 tsp. baking soda

2 cups water
2/3 cup vegetable oil
1 tbsp. white vinegar
2 tbsp. vanilla extract

In a large mixing bowl, combine flour, cocoa, sugar, salt and soda. In another bowl, mix together water, oil, vinegar and vanilla. Add wet ingredients to dry ingredients. Using an electric mixer, beat until smooth; batter will be very thin. Place liners in a muffin pan. Fill 2/3 full with chocolate batter. Drop 1 teaspoonful cream cheese mix in the center of each cupcake. Bake at 350° for 30 to 35 minutes. Cool on a wire rack. Can be frozen up to 2 weeks.

Makes 12 to 18 cupcakes

Ann Rhudy, Hokie Mom
Christiansburg, VA

Key Lime Bars

These bar cookies freeze well. If you are feeding a crowd, double the recipe and use a 13 x 9 pan.

Bottom layer:
1/2 **cup butter, softened**   **1 cup sifted all-purpose**
1/4 **cup powdered sugar**   **flour**

Preheat oven to 325°. Using an electric mixer, cream butter. Gradually add flour and sugar. Mix well until dough is formed. Place dough in an ungreased 8 x 8 pan and pat down evenly. Bake for 20 minutes, or until light golden brown. Remove from oven. Set aside.

Key lime layer:
2 eggs   **3 tbsp. bottled Key lime**
1 cup sugar   **juice**
2 tbsp. all-purpose   **Grated rind of 1 lime,**
flour   **Key lime if possible**

In an electric mixer, beat all ingredients together; mixing well. Pour over bottom layer *(note: bottom layer does not need to be cool)*. Bake for 25 minutes at 325°, or until center is set. Remove from oven, cool completely. Sprinkle with powdered sugar and cut into bars.

Makes 9 bars

Fresh Apple Cake

This is a wonderfully moist, fall weather cake. It is sturdy to travel with, but tender to slice.

1 1/2 **cups all-purpose flour**
1 1/2 **tsp. baking powder**
1/4 **tsp. salt**
2 **cups sugar, divided**
1/2 **cup butter, softened**
2 **tsp. vanilla extract**
1 **(8 oz.) pkg. cream cheese, softened**
2 **large eggs**
2 **tbsp. cinnamon**
3 **cups peeled and chopped Granny Smith apples**

Preheat oven to 350°. In a medium bowl, combine flour, baking powder, and salt. Set aside. Using an electric mixer, cream together 1 1/2 cups sugar, butter, vanilla, and cream cheese, until light and fluffy. Add eggs, one at a time until well blended. Add flour mixture to egg and butter mixture until blended. In a small bowl, combine remaining 1/2 cup sugar and cinnamon together. Take 2 tablespoons of sugar and cinnamon mixture and mix with apples. Fold apples into batter. Grease a 9-inch springform pan. Pour batter into pan, and sprinkle remaining sugar mix on top of batter. Bake at 350° for 1 hour, or until toothpick comes out of center clean and cake pulls away from sides of pan. Cool cake completely on a wire rack. Remove sides of pan. Cut gently using a serrated knife.

Makes 12 servings

Brown Sugar Pound Cake

3 cups all-purpose
   flour
1/2 tsp. baking powder
1 1/2 cups butter,
   softened
2 cups light brown
   sugar

1 cup sugar
5 eggs, room
   temperature
2 tsp. vanilla extract
1 cup milk, room
   temperature
1 cup chopped pecans

Grease and flour a 10-inch tube pan. Mix together flour and baking powder; set aside. Using a mixer, cream butter until light and fluffy. Add sugar and mix well. Beat in the eggs, one at a time. Stir in vanilla. Alternately add flour mixture and milk, mixing just until combined. Stir in the chopped pecans. Pour batter into prepared pan. Bake at 325° (do not preheat) for 1 hour 15 minutes, or until toothpick inserted into center of the cake comes out clean. Let cake cool in pan for ten minutes. Turn out onto a wire rack and cool completely.

Makes 16 servings

Coconut Cream Cheese Pound Cake

3 cups all-purpose
   flour
1/4 tsp. baking soda
1/4 tsp. salt
1 cup butter, softened
1 (8 oz.) package cream
   cheese, softened

6 eggs, room temperature
2 tsp. vanilla extract
3/4 cup shredded
   coconut

3 cups sugar

Grease and flour a 10-inch tube pan. In a medium bowl, combine flour, soda and salt. Set aside. Using a mixer, cream together butter, cream cheese and sugar. Beat in eggs, one at a time. Slowly add in flour mix, stirring until just combined. Fold in vanilla and coconut. Pour into tube pan. Bake at 325° (do not preheat) for 1 1/2 hours, or until a toothpick inserted into the center of the cake comes out clean. Cool for 10 minutes. Turn out onto a wire rack and cool completely.

Makes 16 servings

RECIPE INDEX

Recipe Index

Audrey Lynn Publishing, LLC
P.O. Box 10041
Blacksburg, VA 24062

Please send ____copies of
Tech Tailgates   @ $18.95 each _____

Postage and handling   @ $ 3.95 each _____

Virginia residents add   @ $ 0.85 each _____

                                          Total _____

Name _____

Address _____

City _____ State_____ Zip_____

Make checks payable to *Audrey Lynn Publishing, LLC*

Audrey Lynn Publishing, LLC
P.O. Box 10041
Blacksburg, VA 24062

Please send ____copies of
Tech Tailgates   @ $ 18.95 each _____

Postage and handling   @ $ 3.95 each _____

Virginia residents add   @ $ 0.85 each _____

                                          Total _____

Name _____

Address _____

City _____ State_____ Zip_____

Make checks payable to *Audrey Lynn Publishing, LLC*